What people are saying about

Adding To Your Financial Portfolio

"...so simple it's actually enjoyable...investing really is for everyone..." ..." Manny Carbahal, CPA, Davis, CA

Building Your Financial Portfolio On $25 A Month (Or Less)

"...truly makes investing enjoyable..." Patty Lydon, Bookkeeper, Atlanta, GA

"...inspiring..." Pamela Hull, Financial Manager, Los Angeles, CA

"...a good solid book for novice...makes a lot of sense..." Patrick McKay, Sr., Postal Worker, Independence, MO

Getting Your Dream Life: Career, Sex & Leisure

"...positive, powerful and packed with good ideas for success in life **and** in business..." Barbara A. Scott, President, Zenar Books, CA

Getting A Free Education: The Key To Your Career

"...clearly written, delightfully easy to read...practical and attainable advice..." Sacramento Public Library

ADDING TO YOUR FINANCIAL PORTFOLIO

©1998

B. R. Christensen
E. S. Christensen

EFFECTIVE LIVING PUBLISHING
P. O. Box 232233
Sacramento, CA 95823

Published by Effective Living Publishing
P. O. Box 232233, Sacramento, CA 95823

Copyright ©1998 by B.R.Christensen and E.S.Christensen

Cover design by Tamara L. Dever, TLC Graphics,
Orangevale, CA

This publication is designed to provide accurate and
authoritative information in regard to the subject matter
covered. It is sold with the understanding that the publisher
is not engaged in rendering legal, accounting, or other
professional service. If legal advice or other expert
assistance is required, the services of a competent
professional person should be sought.

Library of Congress Catalog Card Number: 96-091018

ISBN: 0-9643699-5-8

TABLE OF CONTENTS

INTRODUCTION

Our first book on investing, *Building Your Financial Portfolio On $25 A Month (Or Less)*, won the 1998 Best Business Book award and has become a national best-seller. Our purpose in writing this sequel is to help those of you who read that book (or attended one of our seminars) to advance your knowledge of investing even more, past the beginning stage and on to the intermediate level. We had no intention of writing a follow-up to our first book. However, we found that fully half of our readers and seminar participants were asking us for a good book to help them learn more about investing. We looked at the available material and found that, although there were plenty of lengthy and complicated books for the advanced investor, there was no book for the intermediate investor.

Adding To Your Financial Portfolio is meant for the investor who enjoyed our first book (or seminar) so much that they want to learn more about investing by advancing to what we call the intermediate level of knowledge. However, it is not absolutely necessary to have read the first book in order to use this one, keeping in mind that we recommend all investors keep the majority of their savings in the safe and high growth stocks we talk about in *Building Your Financial Portfolio On $25 A Month*.

This book is for the individual, regardless of age, race, sex, or anything else, that enjoys the fast pace of the stock market and wants to spend some time each day reading, listening, and learning. We will teach you step-by-step how to research an industry and companies within that industry in order to know when to jump into the market and when to jump out again using all of the information that is available to any citizen to make these decisions.

By using this more advanced method, you will be able to buy and sell stock that will give you more growth in the value of your purchase in a reasonable length of time (18 months or more). Thus, rather than see a 100% or more average increase in value over 10 years (as in the previous book), you can look for investments that might grow 150% or more in without having to wait for five or ten years.

In the first book, we taught you how to invest on very little money. In this book, because we are looking for short-term large-growth investments, you will need to buy $500 to $1,000 at a time in these investments in order for it to be cost effective. Nevertheless, you can still make a personal decision to invest $300 or $400 realizing that your gain will not be quite as much.

Is this method as safe as the method used in *Building Your Financial Portfolio*? A little more risk is involved, but not much. We will show you how to judge the risk involved so that you can invest according to how much risk you are willing to take. That is, how to find low priced stocks that you believe, through your research, is going to grow at a fast rate for a period of time before faltering due to international, national, industry, or company events. However, remember that you can also use this method of investing to purchase stock in very safe companies that are more cyclical but would not cause losses to you even if you lost track and did not sell at the appropriate time, but rather turned them into long-term investments.

We know to never say never, but we truly believe that we will <u>not</u> be writing a sequel to this book because there is already an abundance of books available for the advanced investor, even if they are difficult to read, that talk about places to put your money that we personally would never recommend to anyone or use ourselves. In the bibliography, you will find many advanced books annotated as to which ones we feel might be the most helpful to you. We know that not everyone finds investing interesting (in fact, to some people it can be quite boring), but we know that some of you will find it fascinating and fun and will continue to grow in knowledge.

Authors always use this section for thanking the people who have helped them create this book. We have to thank our thousands of seminar participants who asked the right questions and, thus, helped us see what you need and want to know. Also, without your letters and verbal thanks to us, we would not have been able to help so many other people learn to safe-guard their own financial future. On top of that, we heartily thank our son, David Christensen, for all of his support and many hours of computer help. We would also like to thank all the members of the Sacramento Publishers Association who not only put their trust in Bobbie as their President, but who were always there with words of thanks and encouragement. And without encouragement, where would any of us be? We only hope that we can spend the rest of our lives helping others to take charge of their own lives, follow their own dreams, and, in the final chapter, help others along the way.

Bobbie and Eric Christensen
September 1998

1. What's The Method

Let's get right down to brass tacks. In the previous book, *Building Your Financial Portfolio On $25 A Month (Or Less)*, we showed you how to find very safe secure investments that are growing an average of 100% or more a year (over a five to ten year period), how to invest without paying all those broker fees and expenses, and how to spend just an hour or so a month doing it. In other words, it was for the person who had no desire to become an expert in the investment world but still wanted to see their money grow (the fun part of it). It was also specifically written so that anyone from 13 years old to 90 could easily understand it and actively use it.

This book is again written for any age group but also specifically for the person who has found the stock market exciting and, hopefully, even fun to participate in. These people want to know more and are willing to spend more time doing it (kind of like an enjoyable hobby).

Therefore, with this method, we will show you how to find a trend in the national or international market place, how to track that trend, how to research that particular industry as well as the individual companies within that industry, what to watch for to know when is the best time to buy into that particular stock, and, of course, when is the best time to get out! Obviously, getting a high return on your money means staying away from mutual funds so you need to learn how to chose that right company and at the right time.

Along the way, we will answer a lot of your questions about other investments and terms that you do not necessarily need for this method, but that you may want and need to know about. If a particular term that we use is unfamiliar to you and is not explained in that particular section, please check the GLOSSARY section in this book. Please bare in mind that this Glossary is not intended to be a complete compendium but rather a compilation of terms that the intermediate investor might want to know and understand.

Here is a personal example to show you what we mean when talking about jumping in and out of the stock market (short-term investing). In the early 1980's, the Mideast was heating up (international event) and all the news media was talking about a possible oil embargo (the industry). Eric, knowing nothing about the oil industry other then how to pump gas into his car, decided this was worth looking into. He spent six months reading everything he could about it and talking to people in the know (research) to become an "expert" in the field. He spent several hours every day (including weekends) doing this. In the course of his research, he was looking at the individual companies also and found Exxon to be the strongest one. By doing this research that allowed him to make a well-informed decision, we bought and held $1500 worth of Exxon stock for 18 months. It tripled in value in that time. Would you like to see your money grow by 300% in just 18 months? We will be giving you even more examples as we go along in this book.

As you can see, our two methods of investment, short-term and long-term, should be used together. That is, there will not always be a situation going on that would warrant your taking a higher risk with several hundred dollars of your hard-earned money. Therefore, you will still want to do your regular monthly investing and work on building up a safe long-term portfolio. But, if you are truly interested, you can spend an hour or more every day looking for the right time and place to make a short-term investment that should provide your portfolio with faster growth during a shorter period of time.

In order to do all of this, there are certain things you need to be willing to do. First, you have to be willing to devote your **time** to doing the required research and to following the market every day. However, just being willing to do that is not enough because you will soon tire of it. You need to actually *enjoy* doing it. If you have been using our long-term investment strategies, then you should already know whether you really want to spend that extra time on this. If you have not been using our $25 a month method of investing, then the only way for you to tell if you actually enjoy everything that goes along with short-term investing is to try it. However, please understand that we strongly feel that everyone should have a long-term investment plan in place to protect your future and use short-term investing only when appropriate.

Second, you need to have the **guts** to invest your hard-earned money into something that might not work. This method of short-term investing does have more risk involved. What if the industry you thought was going to take off didn't? What if you bought too late and sold too early and made no profit at all? Some people are just born with more patience then others and are, therefore, less likely to make mistakes. But let's face it - - the majority of people will occasionally make a mistake using this method. However, if you have found the patience to invest $25 each month in a longer and slower (but safer) buildup of your savings, then you will probably have the perseverance and, sometimes it seems like, the nerves of steel necessary for short-term investing.

Therefore, third, you have to decide how much **money** you are willing to invest knowing that you might make a mistake. In the previous book, we showed you how a person with very little money could buy one share of stock and keep adding a few dollars each and every month to it in order to turn that investment into a big savings. However, in this book we are talking about trends, cyclical businesses, special opportunities and investing for the short-term (as opposed to the previous book using long-term investments). With short-term investing, you will not have time to slowly build up your investment so we will be talking about very different criteria for your choice of stock as well as more money. How much more money? Probably not less than $500 (although you can use even less) up to an amount you can feel comfortable possibly losing if you do make a mistake. Certainly no one wants to or feels really comfortable loosing even $500. But you also do not want to lose so much that it will affect your families life style. And you don't want to invest if you are going to make yourself sick from worrying about your investment. Being very conservative people, when we find a good investment like this, we usually invest less than $1,000. However, you will notice that, contrary to what you might believe, it is not mandatory that you have $1,000 in order to start investing. In Chapter 5 we will be discussing how to use a discount broker which allows you to invest less than $1,000 as well as chose your own stock.

Fourth, you need to be **persistent** for two reasons. One is that there will not always be the correct opportunity available to use this type of investing. That is, there might not be a situation worth taking advantage of for months or even, occasionally, years. Or, you do the research but cannot find any company within that growth industry that looks like a really good investment. Therefore, you want to keep most of your savings in the market using the methods in the previous book and wait for the *correct time* to make these occasional short-term investments.

The second reason for being persistent is that, if you lost money on your first attempt at this type of investing, you have to decide whether to try again or to just stick with a safer long-term investing approach. Keep in mind that it is estimated by Investors Business Daily that the "expert" stock broker or analyst loses money on a third to a half of their suggested investments. Assuming that you care a lot more about your money then a stranger does, you will probably take more care in making your decisions and, thus, make "good" decisions. Remember, gamblers do not make a profit, but professional gamblers only bet on a sure thing.

With these four attributes in mind, who should be using this method of investment? Probably not a teenager without the parents permission. Yes, we have seen teenagers who understood the stock market much better then their parents but still feel an adult should be involved. Also, teenagers (who should be saving for educational purposes) should only be investing in long-term capital appreciating investments. However, any adult who feels they can afford to invest a few hundred extra dollars can do this. In fact, that is one of the great things about the stock market - - it is unbiased. That is, it doesn't matter what age you are, whether you are male or female, what race or religion you are, or even how much money you have, because all investors are treated exactly the same and will get the same percentage of gain no matter what dollar amount they start with. What matters is your willingness to do the necessary work (nothing is free in this world) and your tolerance for a higher level of risk in your life. Yes, some people actually get a thrill out of having more risk, but this book is not for gamblers. Unfortunately, a gambling personality can take our relatively safe methods of investing and go overboard, taking more and more risk, and end up losing everything he started with. Both of our investing methods are meant for sensible people who understand the need to provide for their own financial security. And please note that we use the term "he" throughout this book only for convenience sake.

2. Why Invest In The Stock Market?

The American democracy with its free enterprise system gives us many choices in life. Not only do we have huge selections in our stores and the choice of living anywhere we want to, but we also get to choose our own life styles and even our own values. The methods of saving or investing money in this country are as varied as the choice of shoes to wear.

We chose the stock market for investing because, if used correctly, it is historically the safest place and offers you the largest rate of growth for your money. Since 1900 stock prices (or the market) have gone up more than they have gone down *and* the good strong markets (called bull markets) have lasted longer than the losing markets (called bear markets). So, by investing in the stock market, the odds are in your favor to make money.

The stock market has risen on average 2 out of every 3 years since the crash of 1929. In fact, historically, the individual investor, who carefully chooses which companies to invest in and sticks with the large strong companies, has done better in the market than the so-called professional analysts and brokers. In fact, we find it interesting that most analysts and brokers have never worked in the industrial sector of our country. Most went directly from school into the investment industry. How well can they understand the business and industrial world that they have never participated in? They have the theoretical knowledge but not the hands-on type of knowledge that you have.

In order to keep our market safe, however, we need to encourage individuals to invest directly in the market rather than through group efforts such as mutual funds. Because of the massive amounts of advertising done by funds (which are part of your pension plans and IRAs also), these plans have huge dollar amounts to invest which means that they can actually influence the price of stock to their own advantage. If just one brokerage decides, for whatever reason, to sell off all of their shares in a particular company, it can have a highly visible effect on that company's value. If other brokerages decide to follow suit (this is the herd instinct) and sell off their shares of that company, the effect can be very distressing.

There are also efforts being made in Washington, D.C. to change our social security program to allow you to have a choice of how to invest a part of your wage deducted social security. However, the choices they are talking about include having a certain number of mixed funds available or, in other words, more mutual funds that will be controlled by the analysts and brokers. Hopefully, our Congresspeople will decide that we Americans are intelligent enough to do our own investing without having brokers use our retirement money to influence the market place for their own interests. Yes, brokers and analysts do make published recommendations that do affect the market prices, even if only temporarily. However, the more individuals that are actively investing their own money and the fewer fund managers involved, the safer and more stable the market will be.

These reasons are probably of the most interest to you personally. But don't forget that, when you invest in American companies, you are helping our economy to grow stronger in the world and securing more jobs for you, your children, your friends, and those you don't want to have to support on welfare. If you ever have doubts about the benefits to all of us of capitalism, remember that the United States has the largest number of rich people of any country - - and those people are investing in our stock market! If you fail to invest, you will not be one of those people and you will have no one to blame but yourself. Capitalism is what allows you the right of starting your own business or investing in, and thus becoming part owner of, another business. This creates more jobs for everyone (including your children) and more financial strength for the country you live in.

Before we get into our particular method of investing for the short-term, we should talk about some of the other choices you have.

Savings Account: You can put any amount of money, even just $1, into a savings account and you will receive interest on your money. The interest rate changes with changes in the Federal Reserve's interest rates. This is the place for money that will be used in a very short time period such as saving $100 to buy your first share of stock (see *Building Your Financial Portfolio*) but is a waste of your money for anything else in that the interest rate you receive will not keep up with the rate of inflation (currently at about 3% a year).

Certificate of Deposit (CD): This is investing a large amount of money (at least $1,000 but usually much more) for a certain number of years (one year and up) at a guaranteed rate of return. The more money you put in and for a longer period of time, the higher your return. You will not lose money in your savings account or in a CD but, considering taxes, you will not be able to keep up with inflation either. Typical current rates are 4% for one year or 5% to 5½% for two or more years.

Bonds, Notes, and Treasury Bills: A bond is typically a longer term investment with a specific maturity date (from one to ten years) requiring at least $1,000. They are sold by our governments (Federal all the way down to local) to offset debt, are guaranteed, and usually have no local or state taxes. However, bonds do not grow as a business can grow and expand and, therefore, cannot keep up with the rate of inflation either.

Currently, you will only be seeing a 5% or slightly higher rate of return on these. If the bond is making only 1% over the inflation rate of 3% a year and each year you own that bond the inflation rate is another 3%, you cannot make any profit. Brokers will usually suggest transferring your money from the stock market to bonds when the market is dropping quickly so as to keep your money safe. You will not gain anything on your money but you will not lose anything either. However, we personally feel that, when Wall Street becomes a bear market, you will still get a much better return on your money by staying in the market but only in the "safe" companies (see previous book) and only for the long-term, thus waiting out any down periods.

Mutual Funds: There are many, many different types of funds and the number is growing. Mutual Funds are offered by an investment fund company (the merchandiser), sold to you by a stock broker (the salesman), and require very large investments (much larger then the $1,000 you put in). That is, a brokerage firm receives fees and expenses (in one form or another) from you to invest your $1,000 into a particular mutual fund.

Their purpose is to make money. They do not use their own money but rather the investor's. The brokerage must pay for the trades, accounting, etc. entailed with mutual funds and they charge fees and expenses to do this for you. Therefore, a broker wants thousands of investors, each contributing $1,000 into the fund and contributing fees and expenses into their own pocketbooks. And remember that they will still get their fees and expenses whether the fund makes money or loses money for you. How do they collect these fees and expenses from you?

Stock brokers have found mutual funds very lucrative in that, just like in the grocery store, they can offer you a wide choice thus attracting more shoppers...I mean, investors. A **discretionary (or wrap-fee) account** means that your chosen stock broker will make all investment decisions for you. When you invest in a fund you will be paying fees either on a continuing basis that can vary from 1% to 3% a year plus expenses, or with a fee at the purchase date and expenses on a continuing basis, or on-going expenses with a fee when you decide to get out of the fund. In other words, one way or another, you are paying the broker. **No-load funds** are purchased directly from the mutual fund company and have no sales charge but do charge fees. There can also be a redemption fee at the end.

With some funds the redemption fee is canceled after you have been in it for 6 to 12 months and is used to keep investors from jumping from one fund to another (some redemption fees are never canceled). **Load funds** have a sales charge and can be either front-end (charges are paid at time of purchase) or back-end (charges are paid at time of redemption) the idea being that you will make so much money from your investment that you will not mind paying those fees (although you probably will mind if the fund loses your money and you still have to pay up at the end). An **open-end fund** means that more shares can be put into the market place by the mutual fund company thus affecting what price you will get for your shares. In **closed-end funds**, there are a fixed number of shares in the fund so that your selling price is affected by supply and demand, not by the mutual fund company itself.

If you believe that you will not be charged anything to join a mutual fund, please read the fine print; no broker is going to work for you for free. Unfortunately, some people misunderstand the salesman, do not bother to read the contract, or cannot understand it until it is too late.

Having said all this, there is one exception where mutual funds are a good value for the investor, and that is a **401K Plan** where you are allowed to choose how your fund is invested *and* where your employer picks up the brokerage fees. This is a good employee benefit.

Trading on margin is borrowing the money from the broker in order to buy the stock you want. This can be quite dangerous as in the 1929 crash when not only did the stock market prices collapse but, in addition, most of the investors had borrowed on margin. Thus their purchases were now worth much less, yet they still owed the higher amount that they had bought them at. When they could not sell any other stock at a profit to pay off these debts, they had to sell everything they owned or go to jail. Since 1929, we have been protected by laws allowing an investor to borrow no more than 10% of the value of the stock. Unfortunately, since then, the percentage has been creeping up and is threatening to go all the way back to 90% which could have devastating results in a recession/depression. In any case, as many people have already learned, borrowing of any sort only gets you further in debt (as witness how the credit card age has affected people).

Tied in with this, new bills are being introduced in Congress that would allow brokers to accept credit cards for the purchase of stock. The idea is that you might be paying 18% to 21% interest on your card but getting 23% back on growth. However, by the time you finish paying broker fees and expenses, we doubt that you will have made any money and could end up owing a great deal. And if your particular mutual fund only grew 18%, you would not have any profit. Need we discuss what would happen if your mutual fund made even less?

Index Funds: This is a form of mutual fund wherein you are investing in certain stocks that have historically done well such as an S&P (Standard & Poor) 500 Index. Yes, these have done better then the overall market but, as they are made up of the best performers, why not pick just the one or two very best performers to invest in rather than being overly diversified in 500 different stocks.

Money Market Funds: These usually require a minimum balance of $1,000 or more. The rate of interest for these seems reasonable until you break it down. It is based on the current rate of inflation plus 1% profit for you. Therefore, this can be a place to put your money for a short period of time while deciding how to properly invest it, but do not use it for the long-term. Associated with this is the **Asset-Management Account** which is based on the Money Market Fund (that is, a 1% gain for you) that you are allowed to write checks from (giving you liquidity) and use for buying stocks or trading on margin.

Futures and Options: This involves signing a contract with a broker allowing you to buy or sell 100 shares (or more) of a stock at a specific price and for a specific length of time. In other words, you are gambling on the odds as to whether the price of that stock will go up or down. How confident are you in your crystal ball? This is for gamblers, not investors and, needless to say, we do not recommend this!

Commodities: This is investing in things such as wheat, soybeans, pork bellies, silver, etc. Investing in commodities is betting on whether we will have the right amount of rainfall thus driving prices up. Even our national weather bureau has a major problem with that. Futures trading and commodities are for people who actually work in those businesses and can more aptly judge on a day to day basis what is happening to that particular market. For instance, "Mr. Hershey" might invest in cocoa beans because that is what he handles every day.

IPO or Initial Public Offering: When a company decides that it needs more money, one way to raise the necessary funds is to offer stock in it to the general public (called "going public"). Do you really want to lend money to a business that needs to raise a lot of cash in order to stay in business? If the company uses this cash wisely and in order to grow and expand, it could be a good investment as Microsoft has been (so far). But, again, could even your psychic reader be able to predict this? Osborn Computers went public at the same time as Microsoft and was actually much more highly recommended. But three years later, unable to keep up with the competition, they closed their doors. Historically, the vast majority of new businesses, as well as new public offerings, fail. Even for a gambler, the odds are against you. And quite often when you invest in one of these brand new businesses (not one trying to raise money for expansion) you are actually investing in *a person* who has an *idea*. That is, there is no factory or offices or actual inventory you are buying, but rather just a dream. Yes, these entrepreneurs certainly need support also, but let's leave that kind of financial aid to the very wealthy who will not mind losing a few million dollars.

Bear in mind that most financial managers will recommend that you divide your money up into several vehicles such as stocks, bonds, money-market funds, savings account, etc. We certainly agree that you probably need a certain amount put into a money-market fund or savings account for any immediate emergencies that might arise. However, we recommend that the majority of your savings be in the stock market at all times, no matter what the market is doing. That is, whether the market is up or down, investing in safe long-term investments will be to your advantage. During appropriate time periods and when the right opportunity presents itself, some of your money can be in the stock market in short-term investments.

3. How Does The Stock Market Work?

There are actually several stock exchanges within the stock market that are similar in some ways and very different in other ways and they each serve a purpose for the investor.

The New York Stock Exchange (NYSE), the first stock market in the U.S., was started on the corner of Wall Street in New York City by a group of merchants in 1792. Other exchanges have been added since then such as NASDAQ, the American Stock Exchange, the Chicago, Atlanta and other area exchanges. They were all created as a way to freely bid on the stock in a company. But they are different from one another. We only deal with the New York Stock Exchange and NASDAQ for safety reasons.

The largest is the **New York Stock Exchange (NYSE).** It has more stringent requirements that a company must meet when requesting an initial public offering (IPO), thus it is made up of "safer" companies. You buy or sell stock on the NYSE using a registered broker with a seat on the exchange. When that broker has sufficient orders, they will buy a block of 100 shares of common stock in that company. An interesting note is that the NYSE has real people literally shouting out bids just like in an auction but as though hundreds of auctions were going on at the same time. In fact, the NYSE has become a big tourist attraction and we would highly suggest you make time to visit it when going to New York City.

When a company applies to the NYSE, it asks to be allowed to sell a certain number of shares in their business which is based on how much the company is worth at the time. It must have a market value of at least $40 million and earnings of $2.5 million for the last fiscal year and $2 million for the prior two fiscal years plus meet other stipulations. In other words, you are investing in a company with an operating history and the assets to give you more security. The usual "blue chip" stocks (those that are considered the safest in the market) are usually on this exchange (i.e. IBM, AT&T, Coca-Cola, General Electric, etc.).

Companies listed with **NASDAQ** can vary from very large well-known companies that would meet the above requirements to small companies whose assets consist of a person with an idea. Although these companies may be riskier then those on the NYSE, some companies have shown tremendous growth and gain for their shareholders such as Apple, Intel, Microsoft, and other high-tech businesses that needed to go public in order to grow into huge companies.

NASDAQ is called **over-the-counter** in that you are buying stock directly from the brokers own stock. As most of the companies on the NASDAQ are small, you do have the additional risk of not being able to sell the stock when you want to. That is, a smaller company will not be traded as frequently and you may, therefore, have to wait days or even weeks to sell your stock. Currently there is interest in the fact that most trading of stock is done by computer.

This means that you do not have the mass confusion of the NYSE but it is believed to, at times, slow the bidding process (too many orders coming in by computer to be handled quickly). However, many other exchanges including some foreign ones are using computers. Aside from the historically quaint aspect of people being actually involved in the process, it will be interesting to see if the NYSE ever switches to this method.

Why does the price of stock in a particular company go up and down? Again, it is our free enterprise system at work. When you go into a store, you usually have to pay the price clearly marked on the item. But if you shop for a car, you know that you can barter on the price. If the car dealership is really desperate to get rid of the last of this year's cars, you can offer a lot less for it. If it is a brand new car that has been highly publicized as THE car to own, you will have to pay full price for it or even a premium price.

In the same way, there are several factors effecting the price of a particular stock as well as other factors effecting the overall market which will be discussed in the next chapter.

What effects the price of your stock each day? One factor comes from within the company. The most important consideration is the company's earnings. After all, what you want is for the company to grow, creating more earnings, and making your stock more valuable. One way to calculate this is to look at the earnings per share of stock (**P/E or Price/Earnings ratio**). There are different P/E ratios such as the average annual P/E ratio, the current P/E ratio, the median P/E ratio, and the trailing P/E ratio. Most investors use the average annual P/E ratio to see how the company has been performing. Another thing to consider is whether the earnings are predicted to rise or fall next quarter or next year. But, as this depends on who is doing the predicting, choose your source carefully. We personally recommend using Value Line. Please keep in mind that if a brokerage or analysis firm predicts that the earnings for a particular company should be at such-and-such a level next quarter and then the earnings are lower then predicted, it can have a bad effect on the price of your shares. What is interesting about this is that, obviously, a firm could purposely try to effect the price of the stock for its own interests. Also, in recent years brokerages have tended to predict ever higher earnings then the available information would warrant thus causing the price of a very good stock to temporarily slip when it cannot meet these exaggerated earnings.

What else could effect the price of a stock from day to day? Is there an internal situation at the company that will effect earnings such as a potential labor strike or a change in management by the board of directors? Did the CEO of the company suddenly decide to retire? Did the board of directors just replace the CEO with a proven successful CEO or an unknown and untried person? Did the company just lose their biggest contract or just sign the biggest contract of their career? Did they just announce the closing of manufacturing plants or the adding of new plants and expansion into another geographic area?

Another factor affecting day-to-day stock prices can come from outside the company such as an international or national situation. Is there something that will slow down the materials needed by that company in order to produce their wares? Are there new government policies that will effect their profits? Did a large brokerage firm say something negative about the company to effect the share price? We will discuss these things and more in greater detail in chapter 5.

In other words, something internally or externally (or both at the same time) can happen to the company that might cause investors to buy or sell stock. If good things are happening, then everyone wants a piece and they end up trying to out bid each other (like at an auction) and the price gets higher and higher. If bad things are happening, then everyone wants to sell their stock and, therefore, have to accept less and less money in order to get rid of what they no longer want (as in when you are selling your old car and ask a certain price but are willing to take less just to get rid of it because no one wants that old car). If the items we have mentioned so far seem confusing to you right now, please do not give up yet as we will give more detailed explanations with good working examples later in the book.

With our previous book, we talked about investing in very safe long-term stock that we would hold onto even when prices fell knowing that this company is strong and its stock prices will quickly recover. With this short-term method of investing, we have to be more aware of all the many things happening in the world as well as in the company in order to know when to buy or sell a particular stock. Also, we hope you can now see how a single news item or one statement from an influential market analyst can seriously effect the price of your stock. If you are investing in very safe companies, that statement or news item will have only a passing effect and the price of your stock will quickly (sometimes the very next day) go back up.

However, when investing in even slightly riskier companies, even one statement from an analyst or Congressperson or TV reporter can have a much more severe and long-lasting influence.

These are the basic factors that you need to know about the workings of our stock market. But in order to make an informed decision, you will need to devote part of every day to gathering information from lots of resources. Remember that we believe in keeping investing enjoyable. If doing the research, making your investments, and then watching for the right time to get out becomes too unpleasant (too much like real work), then you will take the joy out of this activity. Your end result should be the pleasure of the hunt and the pleasure of feeling financially secure, not feeling anxious and constantly concerned about whether you are doing the right thing or how you can make even more money. Just keep in mind that greed is called a sin for a very good reason.

4. What You Need To Make A Decision

Now it is time to become very systematic and organized in order to make decisions using your head and not your heart. Virtually everything that happens in the world will effect the economy or some part of it such as a particular business or industry. You need to look at each possible situation and see how you can use that circumstance to your advantage.

Yes, all the other investors and brokers will be doing the same thing, but you have a two very big advantages over them. One is that you care more about your money and your future then anyone else in the world does. Two is that the broker has literally thousands of different companies to keep track of whereas you will be focusing on 2 to 5 companies at a time.

At this point, you need to make the commitment to follow the stock market, as well as international and national news, on a **daily** basis. Although we know of a fanatic who signed a contract with himself to this end, going to such extreme lengths should not be necessary for you. And remember to never jump to conclusions. Taking the *time* to do the proper studying also requires the *patience* to do so. After all, good investing takes persistence and perseverance. We expect you to follow through on each and every step listed, without cutting any corners, before making up your mind. We know of no trend that is set overnight (only fads) but rather builds over a period of time. Otherwise, you will be jumping off a cliff into unknown territory and could get seriously hurt. Being very organized people and wanting you to be just as organized, the necessary steps are in chronological order as much as is possible.

Always keep in mind that, when looking for just the right occasion to buy into a particular company, you could search for months to come to the correct moment when everything comes together and you know that now is the time to jump. But, as the saying goes, getting there should be half the fun.

Step 1 - Your Daily Dose of News

It is essential that you know and understand what is happening **politically** as well as **economically** in the **United States** as well as **worldwide**. Although some short-term investment decisions are based solely on what is happening within a particular company, at this point you are looking for _**overall trends**_ that could offer a certain industry the opportunity to increase their earnings dramatically. Once you find that certain industry, you will concentrate on finding the right company within that industry. In other words, let's start at the top and work our way down.

You have several choices in how you want to gather this information into your brain. The most obvious today is probably television news. Currently, the network news programs are concentrating more on national news, but this changes from day to day as international situations change. When watching the news, keep in mind that you are looking at events not to see how they will effect you and your life but rather how they might effect an industry or a company. Perhaps making the news less personal will also make it less depressing. This may take some getting used to as we do not usually think of news in this impersonal way. Some people have found it handy to write down a short note about each news item and then go back over each point, taking the time to think about each one separately and how it might effect a business or the economy. If you prefer radio news, such as on your way to work, the same applies (although do not write down the news as doing so could be hazardous).

Then again, some people enjoy reading and will, therefore, be checking their daily newspaper and weekly magazines. Your local newspaper (even in a small town) will usually have at least one day each week when they concentrate on business matters, but remember that we are looking at the overall news at this point. The Wall Street Journal is not absolutely necessary so long as you are reading your local (or nearest large city) newspaper. Some people enjoy the weekly news magazines more which are more apt to go into more detail in order to cover a story. And some of you go on the internet every evening to look at everything including the news. Some people who prefer using newspapers and magazines have kept a clipping file of articles that they can continue to study or, if using the internet, you can usually make a print out of what you want to keep.

Whatever source you use, please remember that all news can be strongly influenced by the owner or management of the particular network, station, magazine, or newspaper as well as by the writer or newscaster themselves. Yes, news is supposed to be objective but, historically, these media sources have been owned by individuals or bought by large companies who have a vested interest in promoting certain ideas and information. In other words, be sure to keep an open mind about anything that you read, see, or hear. Just as we need to teach our children to be objective observers of television and ads, we need to learn to be objective also. With everything that you see, hear, or read, you should be asking yourself, "what is the other side of this story?" And there is *always* another side, if not sides. Just as brokers may have a vested interest in influencing your investing, a news source could also have a politically or economically motivated interest. By using many different sources of information, you will be able to find, as Paul Harvey says, "the rest of the story".

What you are looking for are situations that can and probably will influence a particular industry. Obviously, not everything in the news will be of importance to us. Later we will be talking about your becoming an "expert" in a specific industry or industries. At that point you will only have to be thinking about news that will effect those trades. But the following is written for the person who is just beginning to learn about this and, therefore, has not decided what areas most interest him. If you already feel very strongly about and know a great about one or more specific industries, you can start looking for the following pieces of information as they apply to your particular area(s) of expertise.

We cannot possibly foresee every single incident in the world or list every event that has ever effected anything, but we will list things we have seen in the past and seem to be most pertinent to what you will be finding. We will start with **national** issues.

How does the President of our country effect an industry? Is he promoting issues important to his party that might be detrimental, or supportive, to certain industries? This can mean such things as pollution control, many different types of taxes, his positive or negative comments on our economy in general as well as concerning a specific industry or even a specific labor union. His personal life and affairs can and do effect the market as a whole particularly if it could mean his sudden departure from office leaving an unknown entity (the Vice President) to make decisions. The stock market and business people as a whole do not like an unknown future of any sort.

National issues are also effected by what Congress is doing as well as only talking about doing. This can include everyday situations such as raising or lowering social security taxes or some other tax to major decisions such as declaring war or a military action.

What about an announced or possible embargo of a certain country or even a certain item? This leads us into the **international** arena. Again, the President and Congress effect the stock market as a whole as well as individual industries. However, added to this is what the governments of other countries are doing in relation to embargoes, military actions, to say nothing of more drastic measures such as taking over privately owned industries or privatizing formerly government-run industries.

Obviously, some of these things are **economically** related to our business decisions. Are government decisions going to effect our economy over a short or long period of time? A change in just one particular tax law can effect our economy for years, either for good or bad. Is the media reporting that we are going into or coming out of a recession? Or does everything look the same for the immediate future? Did the Federal Reserve announce an increase, a decrease, or no change in interest rates? Are home purchases up or down (taking into account the normal seasonal cycles)?

Did "the market" go up or down today and by how much and why? However, understand that we do not recommend that you make any buying or selling decisions on what the market did in just one day - - usually. For now, we are discussing the general conditions and looking at the broad picture. In chapter 6 we will talk about preparing for seemingly sudden decisions. But as we are looking for trends, we will want to keep track of, in a general way, what the market is doing keeping in mind that, quite often, the market as a whole will not reflect on our particular investment.

Even the economics of other countries effects our investments. Recently, we have seen the near collapse of the Asian market cause a severe drop in our stock market. Why? More and more mutual funds have anywhere from a very few to very many foreign stocks because developing industries can offer a huge potential for very fast growth. However, they also offer extreme risk as no other country in the world is as politically or economically safe as the United States is, to a greater or lesser degree. Do you really want to take that much risk by investing in companies with rocky governments and finances? Yes, someone with money needs to help these countries, but there are people who can stand to lose a big investment like that better then we can. You need to decide for yourself remembering to always make your decisions with your head and not your heart.

Political decisions are far ranging. Our involvement in a military conflict could last for months or years. And we know that whether a Democrat or Republican President is elected will effect our investing, as well as our personal, economics for at least the next four years and probably much longer. Who you support for your local Congressperson, depending on their stated platform, can have a tremendous effect on your investments. Foreign politics can sometimes create a very uncertain world which will adversely effect the market. Whether you like it or not, what happens in China or any country does effect your pocketbook on a daily basis.

Does all of this seem rather confusing? Well, let's try to break down what you are seeing and hearing in the news every day into manageable points to ponder. Exactly what do we want to be looking for in our day-to-day research?

A. Mood - Why on earth would we start with something as ephemeral as mood? Because the mood of the President, of Congress, of Wall Street investors, of the American people, and, most importantly, your mood, will have the strongest effect on your personal investing decisions.

Let's take some situations and see how this works. If we are in a recession with lots of people unemployed and no pay raises in the foreseeable future, chances are the mood of everyone (including yourself) is going to be rather grim. Yes, the President and some members of Congress may be trying to say positive upbeat things, but it may not help the situation. So if virtually the entire country (not counting the occasional Pollyanna) is feeling depressed, no one is going to be investing in the market and driving up the price of stock. In the early 1990's we saw a situation where the economy was improving but the general population would not believe it thus keeping prices depressed much longer then was necessary.

However, if the economy is going great, everyone has a job, you are getting a good pay raise this year, and you can afford to go where you want and buy what you want, then you and everyone else will *feel* like investing in our economy, not just by buying stock in a company, but by your spending on consumer goods and services. However, we personally believe that nothing can ever be gained by being a pessimist because a pessimist will never feel that they can accomplish anything and, therefore, won't. A positive attitude, even in the worst of times, will help any situation. When the market and economy is at the bottom, the only place to go is up!

Something that may surprise you is that any discussion of a possible military conflict will actually have a good effect on our economy (although it may be depressing to you personally to even think about it). The fact is that war creates more jobs with higher wages. This is a good time to again point out that you must always invest with your head and not your heart. You may not approve of the military action, but you must be realistic and be aware of how it will effect your investing and, therefore, your economic future.

Mood is so important that it will actually be reported on by the media. You may have heard the saying, "life is what you make of it", so let's all keep good positive thoughts!

B. Interest Rates - At least this piece of news will be much easier to understand than what mood you are in! You will always want to be watching for any change in the interest rates as announced by the Federal Reserve. The Federal Reserve System was created by Congress in 1913 to make emergency funds available to all the banks that were closing their doors. In other words, they were and are lending money and must, therefore, set the interest rate that they will be charging for these loans. That is, your local bank needs money to lend to borrowers and they have to pay interest on their loan the same as you do. The Federal Reserve (actually the chairman) will set the rate according to how he wants to effect our overall economy.

Why does he set the rates he does? This is more easily understood if we look at the effect it will have. If interest rates are high, businesses cannot afford to borrow money for expansion and there will be either slow or no growth at all (that means lower earnings for the stock holder). That is, the company does not have the money to *invest* in their own business. If interest rates are low, it is much more affordable to expand your business and make more money which will attract investors driving up the price of the stock. It will also mean dividends being paid to the stock holders. Therefore, you as an investor want to buy stock in a company that is expanding and growing or is about to do so.

Obviously, just having lower interest rates does not guarantee that a company will use the money wisely and create a lot of growth, but at least it is another indication of what is possible.

Thus, the chairman of the Federal Reserve system can effect our economy (and your financial future) by raising and lowering interest rates. If there is no growth and, thus, fewer jobs with lower pay, he can lower the prime interest rate making money more readily available. Not only will the businesses be able to afford what they need in order to expand, but you will be able to afford that new house which means more revenue for the building contractors as well as the lumber industry, furniture and appliance industry, landscaping and gardening centers, etc. In order to meet your demands for these goods, they will borrow money to expand, etc. etc.

The reverse is also true. That is, if the economy gets to the point where inflation is setting in (you have more money so the retailer can charge you more and more which you can afford to pay because you are getting paid more and more), the chairman can raise interest rates making money more difficult to get. These increases and decreases in the primary interest rate are usually in very small increments. That is, you may see or hear that the rate is going up ¼% (say from 5% to 5¼%), but even this small amount will start having an immediate effect on the economy. In fact, the very next day you will see the effect on the stock market as it goes up or down. He will continue to raise the rate or keep it steady depending on whether it is controlling our economy enough to keep things on an even keel. Please note that we are not going to get into a discussion of whether this method of control is correct or incorrect. At this point in time, it is a fact of life that we have to live with and should, therefore, make an effort to understand.

The desired effect is to try to keep our economy on a healthy and level keel without going into a deep recession or an astronomical inflation. But, when it comes to making an investment decision, even a slight change in the interest rate is very important. If you cannot afford a loan for your major purchases such as a house or car, then those industries will not have the demand and earnings will fall causing layoffs and shutdowns, creating unemployed workers who cannot afford to buy anything either. This round robin explanation may be sounding silly to you, but it is what has been going on since cavemen first learned to trade a spear for a piece of meat. So do pay attention to the interest rate and to whether it indicates more expansion and growth for our economy or whether we are pulling in the belt and slowing growth.

C. Corporate Earnings and Management - Remember that right now we are looking at events that will have an overall effect on our investing. However, you will see corporate earnings and management discussed throughout this book as it has the greatest effect on our investing strategies.

Keep in mind that corporate earnings effect how many jobs are available out there and how much the workers get paid which in turn effects how much they can spend which effects other industries. If that sounded like we were going around in a circle, we were. We all effect each other every day. Thus, when you are checking out the daily news, it is important to note whether corporate earnings *overall* are going up or down.   If corporate earnings are going up, it means the economy is strong and healthy.   But, if earnings are going down, that means the economy is slowing down - - which makes the price of a share of stock drop - - which can also mean it is a good time to buy stock.   If the price of a share of stock in a good company goes down, it is a good time to go "sale" shopping.   Right now though, we are looking for *overall* trends.   We are not making any investment decisions at this time.   While checking out the news, you want to be aware of which way corporate earnings are going or what the "trend" is.

In the title of this section, we also mentioned "management".   We will be talking much more about management later.   For now though, keep in mind that what kind of management a company has (i.e. proven good leadership or proven continuous mistakes) will effect its earnings.   Simply put, good management will make good decisions that help the company and bad management can drive a company out of business.   More about this later.

D. Stock Market Cycles - Everything in life has cycles including the market.   And there are lots of different cycles. In fact, as the job title of "financial analyst" grows, we are seeing more and more cycles as these experts attempt to develop their own special incomprehensible methods.   But there are certain cycles that are well proven throughout history to have an effect on our investing.   And all businesses are effected by cycles.

The time of year is the most obvious cycle but *not one that we use*.   Seasonal cycles can vary for different industries.   That is, if you hear in the news that housing starts (that is, the building of new houses) are down, before you panic, look at the time of year. Throughout the northern half of the United States, there are few housing starts during the winter because of snow so, obviously, starts will be down. Industries such as toys and electronics (grown-up toys) should be up when we are approaching Christmas. Therefore, just hearing that electronic sales are way up does not mean you should go out and purchase stock in those companies if it is only a very short cyclical event. Again, keep in mind that we are looking for short-term investment opportunities but not just 2 months long!

There are also natural cycles that will cover several years at a time (thus meeting our short-term criteria). One such cycle is based on **our presidential election years**. Based on our economy since the 1800's, the first two years of a President's term are not as strong as the last two years because the market will be wary of what this new person is going to do at first. Then, during the last two years of his term, the market will understand where he intends on taking things. But, of the last two years of his term (in which the market will be stronger) the third year is actually the strongest. By the fourth year, we are again wondering what the future will bring - - more of the same President and Congress or a complete change in direction. In other words, what administration is in office seriously effects your everyday economics to the point of determining whether you will have a job next year! Please vote.

Another important cycle is the **business cycle** or when the economy is growing and when it is contracting. We have already discussed some of the things that help create a growing economy such as low interest rates, strong government, growth in corporate earnings overall, etc.

What about a contracting economy, currently referred to as a **recession**? The official description of a recession is when the **gross national product** (GNP), after being adjusted for the current rate of inflation, declines for two quarters in a row. That is, our total created goods and services that we are producing, adjusted by the rate of inflation, continually decreases for 6 months.

Historically, once the American economy gets into a growth period, it will continue to expand for three or more years. When the economy starts to slow down, it will do so for about 18 months. Certainly these numbers will vary by a few months but have proven accurate over the long haul. In other words, just when you personally are getting discouraged about the economy, count the months and realize that the turn around is on the way. Also, do not confuse a recession with a correction. Yes, the stock market will be going down during a recession AND during a correction, but the correction is very temporary lasting one day or even a few months with ups and downs during those months.

Another traditional definition for recession is when the stock market has dropped a total of 20% (a correction, on the other hand, is a drop of 10% to 20%). However, keep in mind that these are bench marks. In real life, the mood of stock brokers and, to a lesser extent, the mood of the general population (two totally different entities) will have the biggest effect on whether our economy drops into a recession.

E. International Events - It does not matter whether you personally are an isolationist (a person who wants to keep out of the affairs of others), the fact is that events happening in other countries do effect our economy and, therefore, our lives. Some things have a very small effect such as the election of a new Prime Minister in England (because England is governmentally sound and strong). However, if a government is taken over by force by a terrorist or anti-American affiliated leader, this could mean that certain raw materials our businesses need will be in short supply or American businesses operating in that country could be forced to leave or many other serious consequences. These are the type of international events that can create long-term trends that we need to be watching for to make short-term investment decisions.

If using long-term and short-term in that last sentence sounded like a contradiction, it was not. Let's look at an example. Suppose that a dictatorial government came into power in an oil producing country. Let's say that he is in power for the next 20 years, although at the time we do not know that he will last that long. The immediate short-term effect could be a severe shortage of oil to the United States. Although he is in power long-term, it has a short-term effect because within one to two years we would have found ways to compensate for the shortage. Therefore, this political coup would only effect our short-term investing.

F. Age of Investors - This is a very long-term trend that can take several years to spot. The best way to describe this is to look at the current age of investors. Right now, the group of Americans with the most money available to invest is the so-called baby-boomers. They are the ones old enough to have accumulated excess income to invest. However, how they invest their money is also very important. The baby-boomers were born after World War

II and grew up during the affluent 1950's. Therefore, they are more upbeat about our economy and interested in more frivolous things such as travel and amusement parks, high-tech entertainment from computers to large-screen TV's, sports and health equipment and food, etc.

Although it will probably be many years before we see the next consumer group (generation X) influencing the market to such an extent, it is important to try to understand how this group (a large and financially secure group) is going to effect the stock market. And don't forget that we have the larger-then-normal baby-boomer group that will be retiring soon. How will their spending and investing change as they retire? Will they take a tremendous amount out of the stock market and thus effect the whole market? Will they continue to spend as freely when they are retired thus helping to keep the current strong economy going longer? No, we do not have the crystal ball working yet, but read as many interpretations as you can about this future factor in order to make your own decisions.

These are the things that you will want to keep an eye on in order to spot upcoming economic trends. Some of these things such as the middle east and oil situations are very short-term and, therefore, require watching the news daily. Some are very long-term such as the baby-boomers retiring that will take even experts years to spot. But they all add up to asking yourself **"what industry looks like it is about to start a period of big (very big) growth"?**

As we said before, you can watch the news daily for quite a long time and not see any clear or very large growth potential. **This book is not about an on-going every day type of investing; it is about finding the occasional**

short-term opportunity. But if you keep watching, eventually all of the right things will happen at once creating a good investment opportunity for you.

For instance, remember our example on page 2. Just before the last Middle East oil embargo, there was a lot of speculation about it in the news. Eric, deciding that this could be an important money-making trend, spent the next six months becoming an expert in the oil industry (how to do that will follow shortly). Plus, during his intensive training, he was looking at all of the companies that made up the oil industry and researching each of those (also to follow shortly). So in six months, we decided this was a good opportunity to get a good buy on some oil stock and had decided that Exxon was the best choice due to strong management, past history, and an excellent research and development program. We bought low, hung on as long as we felt we could, and sold about 18 months later for a 300% increase in our investment. This is the kind of trend you are looking for.

At this point, we would like to stress to you that we recommend investing (and do ourselves) in relatively safe "blue chip" stock. Yes, we are looking for high and fast growth, but we also do not believe in risking everything on very "iffy" gambles. You must become an expert in a particular field so that you are, at the very least, an informed investor. Then you will not be taking unnecessary risk. For instance, if you decide to invest in a volatile high-tech company only because you ASSUME it will continue to be the correct trend, you are asking for trouble. For those of you that might be old enough to remember, think about what happened with the 8 track tape player! Every day on the news you hear of some new "invention" that will make the current state-of-the-art equipment immediately antiquated. The more volatile an industry is, the more closely you must watch it because it will have much more drastic, literally overnight, changes in stock prices.

Supposing that you have spotted a trend in a particular industry that you want to take advantage of but realize you do not know all you need to know about that industry to make a successful decision? You will now go to the next step.

Step 2 - How To Become An Expert In An Industry and Find The Right Company At The Same Time

It is very important, if not crucial, that you only invest in an industry that you understand very well. Otherwise, you could miss events that will mean the difference between making money and losing money. After all, you want the executives of the company you are interested in to be "experts" and know what they are doing, so you as a future part-owner (share holder) of that company must also become an expert.

You may already be an expert in a particular field but, if that field does not really interest you, you might not want to invest in it. That is, you will pay more attention and consequently make fewer mistakes if you find what you are doing is very interesting and stimulating to you. **IMPORTANT - Just because you find a trend that will mean large growth does not mean you have to invest in it. You can and should pick and choose what you want to go after.** Even the highly paid stock exchange analysts are not experts in everything but have one or two industries they specialize in. You should do the same thing. It is very easy to use hind-site and say "gee, I wish I had invested in Microsoft". But what is much more important is to invest in what you know and understand and, therefore, feel comfortable about. It will take a great deal of stress out of the situation (commonly referred to as being able to sleep at night) and prevent expensive mistakes.

Also, contrary to what you may have been told, anyone, including you, can become an expert in anything you want. And it can be relatively easy to do *if* you choose an industry you are interested in. You will quickly become discouraged if you force yourself to do the necessary studying in an area that is totally boring to you. Besides, we truly believe that investing should and can be fun, but only if you feel involved with your investment and enjoy being a part of and feel pride in a particular industry and a particular company.

Again, being very organized people, we want to clearly define the steps necessary to become an expert in a certain field. Always keep in mind that you cannot take shortcuts in this area and must follow each item carefully. Also, as you research an industry, you will be researching the companies involved at the same time and coming to conclusions as to which company offers the best growth potential for your money (thus saving a little time).

A. Read and Listen To Everything You Can - Some may question as to whether this should be the first or second or third step, but we feel it is the easiest. In our free society, you can find written material (and usually lots of it) on every subject imaginable. Yes, there are some publications we personally recommend (and use) more then others. But the more different resources you use, the better your education. However, like most people, we have our time limitations and, therefore, have certain publications and programs we use. Yours may vary from ours.

The Wall Street Journal has always had an excellent reputation for being unbiased. We have found them to be much more questioning of their sources. That is, most business news items originate from a particular company's (sometimes an industry's) public relations or marketing department. However, The Wall Street Journal is more apt to point out where this information came from and, therefore, question its accuracy.

Using The Wall Street Journal is just like reading any other newspaper. You will read the titles of articles looking for items that apply to the industry you are researching rather than trying to read the entire paper. The same is true of other periodicals you will read. There are several business newspapers besides The Wall Street Journal. There are also many business magazines. However, with the magazines you will need to be a little more careful about what you read. That is, they can have their own agenda for writing either good or bad things about an industry and a company. That is, would the CEO of a famous company allow himself to be interviewed if there was a chance of the article being unflattering to him or his company? Therefore, when reading an article, notice whether the information is coming from quotes or are statements being made by the writer.

We will not even attempt to list all of the reading possibilities as you can go into any book store and have a large number of choices. Please remember that some of the best periodicals are carried by your local public library which can save you a great deal on subscriptions. READ AS MUCH AS YOU CAN which should be A LOT. The more you read, the more you will know. Do not limit yourself to a particular magazine just because they agree with your liberal or conservative point of view. It is important to look at all sides of every issue effecting your industry in order to make a well-informed decision.

Also, when you start your reading research, you will want to read past issues of these publications going back at least several months. The more history of an industry you can find, the more you will understand how current events are going to effect your decisions pertaining to that industry. History does repeat itself.

Do not overlook books. Again, go to your library and look at books written about your specific industry (usually pertaining to an incident that effected it in the past). Again, these can have the writer's particular viewpoint expressed, but reading enough books should give you an overall and well balanced viewpoint. For instance, do you think you can really understand the economic changes taking place in China if you do not know the history of the country? The economics may change, but the traditions do not, and those traditions will have a strong effect on how different countries use the same economic policy but with differing results.

Not just extensive reading is enough however. You also need to listen. There are many excellent (as well as not so excellent) shows on TV and radio that will give you a lot of information to interpret. That is, you might be listening to a Sunday morning debate type of show with the Republican view on one side and the Democrat view on the other. Just as when reading the newspapers and magazines, you need to keep an open mind and interpret what you are hearing. The same is true of news programs.

And the same is also true of what you find on the internet. The internet is part of our "instant gratification" society. You want information and you want it now, not in tomorrow's newspaper. But be aware that there are many different sources of information on the internet. One is the web site of a particular newspaper or TV show. Another is the site of an individual person. Then there is the web site of the company or one of the companies within the industry you are researching. And each of these resources will be expressing their own opinion of events. At the risk repeating ourselves, digest all of this information and then make up your own mind.

Reading and listening are the easiest ways to take in a huge amount of information and get you to at least a qualifying position as a well-informed expert. It will also keep you busy enough to understand why you must limit yourself to specializing in only one or two industries! But there is more work to be done.

B. Talk To People - Just as with reading, you are not going to believe everything you are told, right? But talking to real people within the industry you are researching will give you even more information to go on.

But if you are a sales clerk in a department store, how do you even get a chance to talk with someone in the automobile industry? One way is to call on the phone or visit someone in person in order to ask questions and see what their opinion is. This means meeting with people from all different areas of the industry, not just the CEO or marketing people.

For instance, in the automobile industry, you can talk to employees and owners at your local dealerships (including all makes). Yes, you will hear a lot of rumors along with the basic information you need but, over the course of enough conversations, you should see what is real and what is imaginary. Don't forget that the service repairmen have information for you also as well as the secretary who has worked there for 10 years.

To reach the executive level, you will probably have to depend on what you read in the public press. However, if you have done enough research to have some very specific questions, you can write a letter directly to someone within the company, even the president. You may get a reply from the president or it may be from his marketing department but, either way, you will probably get some kind of a reply. This brings us to a very important, and much more difficult, part of your research.

C. Financial Information Gathering - Although you "read" a financial statement, this is much too important and probably confusing to be included with the reading section. Please do not give up now just because you feel accounting is a foreign language. We are going to explain only the necessary things to look for. You can get a copy of a company's annual as well as quarterly reports by mailing a request to them (the home office address will be in the Value Line), phoning for information (ditto Value Line), or looking them up on the web.

There are a lot of things you can and should determine from financials. You will be looking at the recent (last few years) history of a company as well as looking at its future. The balance sheet, along with your previous reading, will also tell you about the management of a particular company.

There are also two different times when it is appropriate to look at the balance sheet. First, if you have found that there is a particular industry that seems to have the potential for a large growth spurt, you will want to start looking at the **Value Line** information for the larger companies within that industry. Value Line is a highly respected, and our favorite, financial research publication. Unfortunately, it is also very expensive but can be used for free at your public library. Although you might consider the Value Line as reading material (and some of it is straight reading), it is geared toward "the numbers". Therefore, we are using it in connection with financial information.

Let's say that, from your reading and listening, you have decided that the "Retail Building Supply (or home improvement) Industry" is really taking off. Perhaps you have read lead articles telling how more and more people in Canada as well as the U.S. are "doing it themselves". Maybe you have also heard stories about individual companies that are experiencing a higher percentage of growth then other companies within the industry. Of course, having heeded our warnings, you have read and listened to all of this and made your own decisions as to what is real and what is coming from marketing departments. Now you need to find out solid facts.

HOME DEPOT NYSE-HD

| RECENT PRICE | 48 | P/E RATIO | 48.0 (Trailing: 57.8 / Median: 30.0) | RELATIVE P/E RATIO | 2.61 | DIV'D YLD | 0.3% | VALUE LINE | 888 |

TIMELINESS	1	Raised 7/17/98
SAFETY	2	Raised 10/18/96
TECHNICAL	2	Raised 9/26/97
BETA	1.20	(1.00 = Market)

2001-03 PROJECTIONS

	Price	Gain	Ann'l Total Return
High	60	(+25%)	6%
Low	45	(-5%)	-1%

Insider Decisions

	A	S	O	N	D	J	F	M	A
to Buy	0	0	0	0	0	0	0	0	0
Options	2	0	0	0	0	0	0	0	0
to Sell	3	0	0	2	1	0	0	0	0

Institutional Decisions

	3Q1997	4Q1997	1Q1998
to Buy	301	339	377
to Sell	303	279	272
Hld's(000)	907833	915031	926394

Percent shares traded: 18.0 / 12.0 / 6.0

LEGENDS
17.0 x "Cash Flow" p sh
.... Relative Price Strength
3-for-2 split 9/87
3-for-2 split 7/89
3-for-2 split 7/90
3-for-2 split 5/91
3-for-2 split 7/92
4-for-3 split 4/93
3-for-2 split 7/97
2-for-1 split 7/98
Shaded area indicates recession

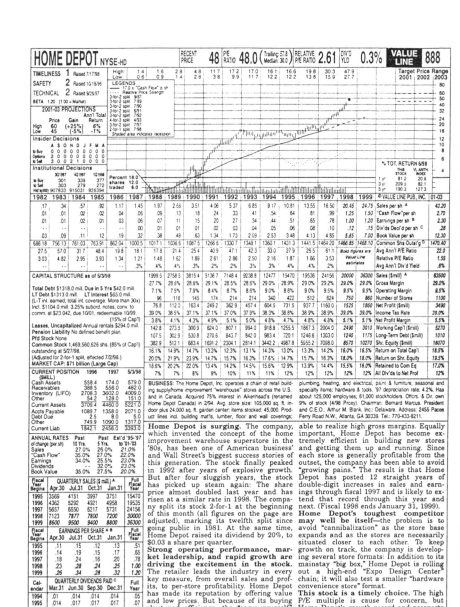

Target Price Range 2001 | 2002 | 2003

% TOT. RETURN 6/98

	THIS STOCK	VL ARITH. INDEX
1 yr.	81.2	20.6
3 yr.	209.5	82.1
5 yr.	190.3	127.3

1982	1983	1984	1985	1986	1987	1988	1989	1990	1991	1992	1993	1994	1995	1996	1997	1998	1999	© VALUE LINE PUB, INC.	01-03
.17	.34	.57	.92	1.17	1.45	1.97	2.56	3.51	4.06	5.37	6.85	9.17	10.81	13.55	16.50	20.45	24.75	Sales per sh A	43.20
.01	.01	.02	.02	.04	.06	.09	.13	.18	.24	.33	.41	.54	.64	.81	.99	1.25	1.50	"Cash Flow" per sh	2.70
.01	.01	.02	.01	.03	.06	.07	.11	.15	.20	.27	.34	.44	.51	.65	.78	1.00	1.20	Earnings per sh B	2.30
..	..	..	..	..	.00	.01	.01	.01	.02	.03	.04	.05	.06	.08	.10	.12	.15	Div'ds Decl'd per sh C	.28
.03	.09	.11	.12	.19	.32	.38	.49	.63	1.34	1.73	2.09	2.53	3.48	4.13	4.85	5.85	7.00	Book Value per sh	12.30
686.18	756.13	761.03	763.91	862.04	1000.5	1017.1	1036.6	1087.5	1266.6	1330.7	1348.1	1360.1	1431.3	1441.5	1464.20	1466.85	1468.10	Common Shs Outst'g D	1470.40
27.5	57.0	31.7	48.4	19.8	18.1	17.8	21.4	25.4	40.9	47.1	42.3	33.0	27.9	25.5	61.1	Bold figures are Value Line estimates		Avg Ann'l P/E Ratio	22.0
3.03	4.82	2.95	3.93	1.34	1.21	1.48	1.62	1.89	2.61	2.86	2.50	2.16	1.87	1.66	3.53			Relative P/E Ratio	1.55
..	..	..	..	..	.3%	4%	4%	3%	2%	2%	.3%	.3%	.4%	4%	2%			Avg Ann'l Div'd Yield	.6%

CAPITAL STRUCTURE as of 5/3/98

Total Debt $1318.0 mill. Due in 5 Yrs $42.0 mill.
LT Debt $1313.0 mill.   LT Interest $65.0 mill.
(L-T int. earned, total int. coverage: More than 30x)
Incl. $1104.0 mill. 3.25% subord. notes, conv. to comm. at $23.042, due 10/01, redeemable 10/99.
(15% of Cap'l)

Leases, Uncapitalized Annual rentals $294.0 mill.
Pension Liability No defined benefit plan.
Pfd Stock None
Common Stock 1,469,560,626 shs. (85% of Cap'l) outstanding at 5/27/98.
(Adjusted for 2-for-1 split, effected 7/2/98.)
MARKET CAP: $71 billion (Large Cap)

CURRENT POSITION	1996	1997	5/3/98
($MILL.)			
Cash Assets	558.4	174.0	579.0
Receivables	388.5	556.0	482.0
Inventory (LIFO)	2708.3	3602.0	4009.0
Other	54.2	128.0	151.0
Current Assets	3709.4	4460.0	5221.0
Accts Payable	1089.7	1358.0	2071.0
Debt Due	2.5	8.0	5.0
Other	749.9	1090.0	1317.0
Current Liab.	1842.1	2456.0	3393.0

ANNUAL RATES	Past	Past	Est'd '95-'97
of change (per sh)	10 Yrs.	5 Yrs.	to '01-'03
Sales	27.0%	26.0%	21.0%
"Cash Flow"	35.0%	27.0%	22.0%
Earnings	34.0%	25.5%	23.0%
Dividends	--	32.0%	23.0%
Book Value	35.0%	28.0%	20.0%

Fiscal Year Begins	QUARTERLY SALES ($ mill.) A				Full Fiscal Year
	Apr.30	Jul.31	Oct.31	Jan.31	
1995	3569	4151	3997	3751	15470
1996	4362	5292	4921	4958	19535
1997	5657	6550	6217	5731	24156
1998	7123	7877	7800	7200	30000
1999	8600	9500	9400	8800	36300

Fiscal Year Begins	EARNINGS PER SHARE A B				Full Fiscal Year
	Apr.30	Jul.31	Oct.31	Jan.31	
1995	.11	.15	.12	.13	.51
1996	.14	.19	.15	.17	.65
1997	.18	.24	.16	.20	.78
1998	.23	.28	.24	.25	1.00
1999	.26	.34	.28	.32	1.20

Cal-endar	QUARTERLY DIVIDENDS PAID C				Full Year
	Mar.31	Jun.30	Sep.30	Dec.31	
1994	.01	.014	.014	.014	.05
1995	.014	.017	.017	.017	.07
1996	.017	.02	.02	.02	.08
1997	.02	.025	.025	.025	.10
1998	.025	.03			

1999.5	2758.5	3815.4	5136.7	7148.4	9238.8	12477	15470	19536	24156	30000	36300	Sales ($mill) A	63500
27.7%	28.6%	28.8%	29.1%	28.5%	28.6%	29.0%	28.9%	29.0%	29.2%	29.0%	29.0%	Gross Margin	29.0%
7.1%	7.5%	7.9%	8.4%	8.7%	8.6%	9.0%	8.8%	9.0%	9.5%	9.5%	9.5%	Operating Margin	8.5%
96	118	145	174	214	214	340	422	512	624	750	860	Number of Stores	1100
76.8	112.0	163.4	249.2	362.9	457.4	604.5	731.5	937.7	1160.0	1525	1850	Net Profit ($mill)	3490
39.0%	38.5%	37.1%	37.1%	37.0%	37.9%	38.3%	38.8%	38.9%	38.9%	39.0%	39.0%	Income Tax Rate	39.0%
3.8%	4.1%	4.3%	4.9%	5.1%	5.0%	4.8%	4.7%	4.8%	4.8%	5.1%	5.1%	Net Profit Margin	5.5%
142.8	273.3	300.9	624.0	807.1	994.0	918.8	1255.5	1867.3	2004.0	2490	3010	Working Cap'l ($mill)	5270
107.5	302.9	530.8	270.6	843.7	842.0	983.4	720.1	1246.6	1303.0	1240	1175	Long-Term Debt ($mill)	1010
382.9	512.1	683.4	1691.2	2304.1	2814.1	3442.2	4987.8	5955.2	7098.0	8570	10270	Shr. Equity ($mill)	18070
16.1%	14.9%	14.7%	13.3%	12.3%	13.1%	14.3%	13.0%	13.3%	14.2%	16.0%	16.5%	Return on Total Cap'l	18.5%
20.0%	21.9%	23.9%	14.7%	15.7%	16.3%	17.6%	14.7%	15.7%	16.3%	18.0%	18.0%	Return on Shr. Equity	19.5%
18.6%	20.2%	22.0%	13.4%	14.2%	14.5%	15.6%	12.9%	13.9%	14.4%	15.5%	16.0%	Retained to Com Eq	17.0%
7%	7%	8%	9%	10%	11%	11%	12%	12%	12%	12%	12%	All Div'ds to Net Prof	12%

BUSINESS: The Home Depot, Inc. operates a chain of retail building supply/home improvement "warehouse" stores across the U.S. and in Canada. Acquired 75% interest in Aikenhead's (renamed Home Depot Canada) in 2/94. Avg. store size: 105,000 sq. ft. in-door plus 24,000 sq. ft. garden center; items stocked: 45,000. Prod-uct lines incl. building mat'ls, lumber, floor and wall coverings; plumbing, heating, and electrical; paint & furniture; seasonal and specialty items; hardware & tools. '97 depreciation rate: 4.2%. Has about 125,000 employ-ees; 61,000 stockholders. Offcrs. & Dir. own 9% of stock (4/98 Proxy). Chairman: Bernard Marcus. President and C.E.O.: Arthur M. Blank. Inc.: Delaware. Address: 2455 Paces Ferry Road N.W., Atlanta, GA 30339. Tel.: 770-433-8211.

Home Depot is surging. The company, which invented the concept of the home improvement warehouse superstore in the '80s, has been one of American business' and Wall Street's biggest success stories of this generation. The stock finally peaked in 1992 after years of explosive growth. But after four sluggish years, the stock has picked up steam again: The share price almost doubled last year and has risen at a similar rate in 1998. The compa-ny split its stock 2-for-1 at the beginning of this month (all figures on the page are adjusted), marking its twelfth split since going public in 1981. At the same time, Home Depot raised its dividend by 20%, to $0.03 a share per quarter.

Strong operating performance, mar-ket leadership, and rapid growth are driving the excitement in the stock. The retailer leads the industry in every key measure, from overall sales and prof-its, to per-store profitability. Home Depot has made its reputation by offering value and low prices. But because of its buying clout and efficiency, the "serve yourself" warehouse format obviates a lot of the need for customer service—Home Depot is able to realize high gross margins. Equally important, Home Depot has become ex-tremely efficient in building new stores and getting them up and running. Since each store is generally profitable from the outset, the company has been able to avoid "growing pains." The result is that Home Depot has posted 12 straight years of double-digit increases in sales and earn-ings through fiscal 1997 and is likely to ex-tend that record through this year and next. (Fiscal 1998 ends January 31, 1999). **Home Depot's toughest competitor may well be itself**—the problem is to avoid "cannibalization" as the store base expands and as the stores are necessarily situated closer to each other. To keep growth on track, the company is develop-ing several store formats: In addition to its mainstay "big box," Home Depot is rolling out a high-end "Expo Design Center" chain; it will also test a smaller "hardware convenience store" format.

This stock is a timely choice. The high P/E multiple is cause for concern, but Home Depot's growth record and prospects justify a considerable premium.

Ben Sharav, CFA   July 17, 1998

(A) Fiscal year ends Sunday closest to January 31 of the following year.
(B) Diluted earnings. Excluding extraord. gain: '85, 1¢.
(C) Next dividend meeting about August 20. Goes ex about September 5. Approx. dividend payment dates: 24th of March, June, Sept., Dec.
(D) In millions, adjusted for stock splits.

Company's Financial Strength A++
Stock's Price Stability 55
Price Growth Persistence 80
Earnings Predictability 100

Value Line is set up so that all of the companies (the ones listed with the stock exchanges) within a particular industry are grouped together. This makes it easy to find the latest issue that covers the Retail Building Supply Industry (as shown on the front cover index) and just flip pages from one company to another. Let's look at the example of Home Depot.

The first thing you should notice is the chart at the top. This is an eleven year history of the company and clearly shows a strong and even history of splits. If the stock splits are fairly evenly spaced on a graph that is continually moving upward, then the owner of this stock is making money. However, for Home Depot, you will see a rather flat period from the beginning of 1993 to the end of 1996 with 1997 showing the price rising again on into 1998. This looks promising.

You will also want to look at the **P/E Ratio**. P/E stands for price (of each share) divided by the earnings (per share). Value Line calculates this for you. As a general rule, you do not want to buy stock if the P/E number is very high (generally over 40). However, with a strong economy and historically high earnings that have no reason to decline in the near future, we do look at companies with higher then normal P/E ratios. Since P/E ratios can vary from one industry to another, you should check all of the companies in a particular industry to see what the average P/E ratio is within that particular industry.

Also, we personally believe that increased earnings is more important to look for then a change in the P/E ratio, particularly if earnings have continued on an upward trend over the past few years. That is, Home Depot has been showing an increase in earnings for many years but with a larger than normal increase through 1997 and into 1998 and with a high P/E Ratio. Now you will want to read the Value Line write-up at the bottom of the page telling Home Depot's recent history and what is predicted for future growth.

Thus we have found an industry trend (home improvement will continue to expand and grow) and a company within the industry that seems to have a very good future when compared with other businesses within that particular field.

We have been talking extensively about how to find future trends effecting an entire industry that could give our investments a nice profit. However, keep in mind that some excellent short-term money-making investments are not directly attached to a specific industry trend. The best way to explain this is to look at the example of Disney. During 1997-98, we have found the entertainment industry as a whole to be a mixture with some companies having slight growth and some showing stagnation. Nevertheless, certain events came together in 1998 to make Disney (just one company out of all the entertainment industry) a "good buy".

First, we know that Disney has been a very strong company for close to 20 years without the usual drastic ups and downs of many other related businesses. Thus Disney is always in the back of our minds as a company to keep an eye on and buy into at the appropriate times and sell at the appropriate times. Second, Disney announced a 3-for-1 split.

A **split** is when the Board of Directors votes to increase your one share to three shares (or whatever the split happens to be). That is, if you owned a share of it, you were now going to have 3 shares. However, along with your original single share growing by 3, the price of each share will divide by 3 going from over $120 (or there abouts) a share down to about $40 a share. So we are looking at an historically strong well-run company in which the price per share will just climb back up and also seeing, directly after the split, bargain-basement prices (buy low and sell high).

But this is not enough to make a decision on. We know that Disney usually has a split just about every 7 years from looking at the chart in Value Line. Thus, we can figure that the price per share will go up again after the split but over a long (7 years) period of time. Seven years is too long to invest in normally for large growth but we saw factors that make us believe that their stock value will increase much faster then that.

So, third, we looked at what is going on with Disney. Well, we know that Michael Eisner has been a very effective CEO for 10 years and plans on staying there. We know that, during recent years, Disney opened a new theme park in Disney World (Florida) that is already showing a profit, that they are revamping Disneyland in California, that they finally turned EuroDisney into a profitable venture, and that they are starting their own cruise line associated with Disney World. We admit some reservations about the cruise line but also know Disney's penchant for marketing and expect that, with their many weekly shows as well as specials on TV, they will probably make everyone in America want to go on a cruise just like the show "Love

Boat" did. In other words, we are looking at a lot of expansion that is already creating higher earnings along with a strong and proven management.

What this all means is that there are two types of vehicles for short-term investing: an industry-wide growth in which you decide which company within that industry will do the best, or a particular company that is set for major growth with its increased earnings even though the industry as a whole is not growing.

So far you have read and heard other peoples opinions about upcoming trends in certain industries and/or expected growth in specific companies. Then, by looking at Value Line, you have read specifically about one company that you think might be a good possibility for big earnings in the coming months. In order to make a final decision as to whether this company is an excellent investment or whether you should go back to your research, you need to study that particular company in more detail.

Now is the time to read the balance sheet. Quite often you will find the most recent annual balance sheet for a company on internet. Most larger company's will be found under their actual name, i.e. www.disney.com. From there you can print out their financials or, if not available on web, email them a request for their Annual Financial Statement. Another way is to get the company's home office phone number off of Value Line and call for the Annual Report. Again, remember that Annual Reports are partly created by a company's public relations department and are, therefore, to be read with caution. However, a publicly held company (that is, one that you can buy stock in on the open market) must have audited financial statements. Therefore, usually the numbers are as accurate as any you will find (not withstanding creative accounting practices).

A large part of the annual report will be written to tell the stock holder (or potential stock holder) how great the company is, what they have been doing during the past year, and all of the wonderful things they plan on doing in the coming year. This is very interesting information and should be read. But, more importantly, you need to read and understand the **Financial Reports**. Moreover, note that you must also read the Notes for that financial statement in order to get explanations that can put a different meaning on the numbers.

The first thing to notice is that figures will be compared with previous year(s) numbers so that you can easily see the timeline of their growth (or decline). Just as when using Value Line, it is important to see the history of the company. What you as a potential investor want to determine from this is:

(1) Is there continued growth in income? Look at the income statement and compare with previous years. Do not make a judgment based on quarter to quarter income as this is too easily effected by annual cycles (i.e. few people buy cars at Christmas time). Read the notes to make sure that a rise in income was not simply created by the sale of assets.

(2) If there was a sale of assets, it should be due to the company reducing expenses and/or "un-diversifying" and going back to their core business. That is, some companies thought that in order to expand they should buy

other companies that had nothing to do with their core business (i.e. a food canning operation buying a pesticide company). They found out the hard way that it is best to stick to the business they know and understand. So if you see this type of sale of assets, it is good for the business.

(3) Make sure there are more assets then liabilities. If not, are you willing to take the risk of not getting anything back for your money if they go out of business. That is, are you willing to lend someone your money if they have nothing they can sell in order to pay you back? For instance, if the company was recently purchased by outside investors (thus becoming more highly leveraged), it will have to make higher sales and profits in order to pay off the loans involved in the purchase.

(4) Expenses should be staying steady, however, increases in Research and Development (R&D) are usually good in that the company will grow from the new products/services, etc. developed. Drug, high-tech, and other quickly changing companies cannot keep pace with their competitors if they do not put a lot of money into continuing research and development. Nevertheless, even steady growth companies must have continued R & D in order to keep ahead of their competitors by creating new products and services as well as to keep increasing their sales and thus their profits.

(5) Sometimes you will have to read the Annual Report carefully to find out if and how much stock the executives of the company own in their own business. Do you really want to invest in a company in which the CEO does not want to invest his own money? Also keep an eye out in your daily reading as well as the financials to see if

any of the officers are suddenly selling off large chunks of stock (not just the occasional sale necessary for life style purchases).

(6) When a company is offering a buy-back (buying back stock from the public) it shows their confidence in their own company. That is, they are generating excess cash not needed for more growth, and they are confident that the shares of stock they are buying back for the company will increase in value for them the same as it will for you. In other words, the company (not just the company executives) is investing in itself. They, like you, believe that they can buy this stock at this price and then release it back to you the public in the future at a higher price thus making a profit.

(7) If the company has been paying quarterly dividends to the share holders, this can also mean an excess in cash. Like you, a company is financially sound when it is paying all of its bills (expenses), continuing to increase its income, and still have money left over. However, it is also good for your investment when a company is using all of its excess cash for further expansion and growth to create higher earnings. Since you are looking for fast and large growth, you should not be interested in receiving dividends. When you reach retirement and want the additional income, you will be looking for large dividends rather than growth.

(8) Have the corporate executives changed during the past year and, if so, why? Retirement and death are acceptable but be wary if they are leaving to join other companies. If it is just one or two people, do their reasons for leaving (higher position, more creative control, etc.) seem legitimate. As with number 5 above, be cautious if the

top executives are "cashing in" or exercising their stock options and selling their personally owned stock on the open market. After all, they may know something is going on behind the scenes long before the investor or the market as a whole does.

(9) Is the company showing very high debt that they will need to pay off in the future. That is, the long-term debt should not be over 50% of their total capital. It should actually be much lower showing a business that does not need a lot of capital. Some businesses can support a higher debt, however, such as fast-food restaurants and consumer products that sell their inventory faster and can thus afford a higher debt. If you are not sure what is considered acceptable debt, compare other companies within the same industry to see if they all show the same percentage of debt or are some much higher or lower.

Now it is time to take all of this collected information and make a decision whether to buy a particular stock, wait awhile longer, or to sell stock you own. To make things a little easier to understand, we will go over when to buy and when to sell in separate chapters.

5. When To "Jump In"

Making a personal decision as to when to buy stock in a particular company is certainly the most difficult part of investing. However, just as in any area of your life, you must make an informed decision by gathering all of the necessary information. This is the point where it becomes very tempting to just hand your money over to a stock broker and let him make all of your decisions for you. Don't do it! Without even considering the additional cost to you for doing this, consider whether you want another person with his own mood swings, job and family pressures, and income expectations handling your money. Do you really want to wonder whether your broker bought or sold some stock for you just because he is going on an expensive vacation and needs some more fees and expenses this month to pay for it? Would you ever recommend to your child that he just hand over his money to a stranger with a verbal promise that he might make money for him - - or he might lose it for him? And, yes, it is historically proven that the individual investor usually makes much better decisions then any broker does.

We suggest that you do not tell your friends and relatives (other then your spouse) about your decisions either because, just as in voting for the President, everyone has very strong reasons (or feelings) about why you should do something else and will try to influence you (do you really need more pressure put on you?). However, when you see the value of your investment go from $35 to $70 a share, it might be time to do a little bragging.

Many people have found it much easier to make a logical decision by writing down their reasons, both for and against, for purchasing this stock. We suggest that you do this. Divide a piece of paper in two halves, down the middle. On the left list the pros and on the right the cons.

First, list how this company's earnings are going to be effected by what is happening nationally and internationally. That is, what did you read that made you even start thinking about this industry? Is there the possibility of a military conflict, is the President or Congress increasing/decreasing taxes on some item? Is a union getting ready to strike? Yes, some of this seems like looking into a crystal ball and trying to foresee the future. But you have the advantage of being able to use the expressed opinions of all the experts you have read and heard in order to come to your own conclusions. That is, you have been reading and listening to everybody rather than going to one stock broker/agent and getting only his opinion.

Do not consider circumstances that are of a very brief nature such as a strike that might only last one week. As an individual investing only a few hundred dollars, you cannot afford the broker fees involved with buying and selling on a daily or weekly basis. Also, brokers are apt to be busy with their larger investors making it difficult for you to buy or sell at the exact moment you want to.

Remember to look for short-term investments that will be beneficial to you for the next 12 to 18 months (possibly longer).

Second, list facts about our own economy that can mean the difference between investing now or waiting. How is the economy? Is it strong with low unemployment and low interest rates? If the economy is currently strong, are there indications of bad times coming such as a rising Consumer Price Index that shows inflation? Are you seeing in-sider articles telling of management selling off their shares? If we have been in a recession for six months or more, are there indicators that the market is about to start rising (lowering interest rates, Dow Jones averages steadily increasing, etc.)?

You do not want to confuse a correction with an actual change in the economy. That is, the stock market could show a decline for several days or even weeks and then go back up again. This is too short a time period for you to be involved with (again, those broker fees can add up very quickly). Some analysts use an advance-decline line (how many stocks are increasing as opposed to losing value) or a relative strength line (how strong is this market compared with other times). However, if you are doing your daily study as required, how the market is doing will be clearly written out as in "the overall market has risen two quarters in a row" meaning things are definitely improving and not being effected by any particular cycle. Keep in mind, however, that an individual company (particularly large companies) cannot adjust quickly to a changing economy and, therefore, even with these factors indicating a change from a recession to a growing economy, the company's earnings will lag behind the market upturn.

Third, look at the facts concerning the particular industry you are interested in.

A. Is it so high-tech that the technology is and will be changing on almost a daily basis? Such fast-change artists are impossible to keep up with when a delay of 4 hours could mean the loss of hundreds of dollars. Please remember that we do believe in keeping risk at a minimum.

B. Do foreign competitors in this industry have the very big advantage of a much cheaper labor force? The garment industry has been in the headlines quite a bit recently with the exposure of their use of such workers. For instance, you could invest in an American clothes manufacturer that has the work done overseas thus producing it at low expense but with a high mark-up in the U.S. stores. This company would be showing good earnings. But what would happen when their practices were disclosed? Would there be even a partial boycott of their goods producing decreasing earnings and hurting the value of your stock?

C. Is this an essential industry that produces what we must have no matter what the economy is doing or is it a non-essential that can be severely effected by a recession. That is, in a recession we do not buy new cars but just keep the old ones running as long as we can (non-essential). But we must continue to buy the fuel for it no matter what happens (essential). Depending on the state of our economy, you might do a short-term investment in either an essential or non-essential industry, but being an essential field would be a definite "pro" item.

D. Most importantly, is this an industry that you understand very well? Have you taken the time and followed all of Step

4 to become an expert in this particular industry so that you can move on to choosing a particular company within this industry? Michael Eisner, CEO of Disney, understands the entertainment industry very well, but how would he do in designing cars? Although some areas of management, marketing, etc. carry over from one field to another, each industry also has its own distinctive ways that can mean the difference between success and failure. It is your job to understand these smaller nuances in order to make an intelligent decision.

E. Is the specific industry you are considering in a growth area such as telecommunications or in a stagnant field such as steel making. A stagnant or dying industry has very little chance of creating a sudden upsurge in earnings.

Fourth, look at the individual company. As you have been looking over the different industries, you have also been collecting information on specific companies. But now you must do the indispensable research on that specific company before making a final decision.

A. Is this company the leader in their field? Are they a possible takeover candidate? If another company decides to buy them, the stock price will go up. This sort of information would be found in the newspapers.

B. Read those financials! Is there strong cash flow with more assets then liabilities? Have the company's earnings been increasing over the past two quarters? Is the increase due to a fad that will quickly disappear or is this a growing new market? If its earnings are not growing, the value of your stock will not grow. Is this company large enough that its stock is being traded on a daily basis thus making it easier for you to sell if necessary? Some small companies may have days or even weeks between any transactions. Watch for companies that do not require a great deal of capital thus creating a product at a very low price that they can sell for a very high price. That is, it doesn't cost the company much to produce glass ware that can produce good earnings.

C. Look at the individual company and read their annual report. Can you tell exactly what their strategy is for the future in terms of expansion and new marketing, products, technology, etc. Is their technology the best available or do other businesses within this industry have more up-to-date facilities and technologies? Yes, you are reading the company's own opinions, but these must be taken into consideration. Do not bother with general statements about future growth but look for specific items such as the recent commencement of building new facilities, an actual increase in R & D money, etc.

D. Are they continuing to expand their research and development? Without this, a company stagnates (no growth). With good R & D, a business can expand its product line, the uses for its products, its foreign sales, and much more.

E. Historically how well has the company conducted business in the past? Does it have good management that has proven that it knows what it is doing? Even a new CEO can be checked out. Find out what company(s) he has headed before and what their results were. Does his history show that he has always worked for you, the share holder? You should see a good history of quarterly dividends (giving money back to the investor). The dividends should not be large as we want a company that is putting money into its own future, but any dividend at all shows that they do want to keep their investors and are not struggling to stay afloat. Did the stock prices of the previous businesses of the CEO increase due to his management? Leadership can and does make a tremendous difference in the success of a business just as your own leadership of your personal financial portfolio can make an immense impact on your own success.

F. What is the company's long-term debt? Just as in your own finances, a lot of debt to pay off is not good. Make sure the company either has no debt or that the debt does not equal more than 20% of its capital or equity. Again, look at Value Line to determine what the average debt is for businesses within this industry and how your selected company compares to the rest. It would be difficult for you to go on an expensive cruise if you had very high debt that you needed to pay off.

G. What is the company projecting for its own future growth and what are other experts predicting? Has it announced new products or services it is developing? Do these products look like good long-term investments rather than fads?

H. Is the stock currently selling at a good price? In order to increase your profit, you want to buy stock that is at an historically low price. Using Value Line, look for a company with a low P/E ratio. Also look at the stock price range for the previous year to see if it is at an historic high, low, or medium figure. If it is at an historic high price, you might want to wait on this particular company or at least look elsewhere. Even if the company meets all other criteria, it will not do you any good to buy stock at a high price and then see it only go up a few dollars before leveling out or declining. In order to maximize your profit, you must buy low and sell high. Yes, we understand that you will probably not buy it at its very lowest price, but if you are indecisive and wait until the price has risen too much, you will get a much smaller profit (assuming that you sell at the correct time).

How low a price are you looking for? That depends on how safety minded you are. You could be looking at a down market where all prices are much lower then they were a year ago, but you believe that one company is going to start climbing again. Or, maybe you want to do some **bottom fishing**. This is when you have researched an industry and happen to come across a company that has fallen on some bad times or just fallen out of favor and is thus very low priced, but that you believe (from your research) is going to forge ahead again. This does not mean that you buy into a company that has never had a good earnings records, has never stood out from the crowd in any way. You are still looking for a company that meets all of the above criteria but, for some reason, has had a bad financial time. For example, Morton Thiokol (now Morton International) was the company responsible for the O-rings that failed in the Challenger space shuttle explosion. Needless to say, even though the rings were used at a temperature below what the Morton Thiokol recommended, that incident did not help their stock any. However, years later they have made tremendous progress, the management is proving that they can cut costs and build earnings, yet their current stock price is only $26 (with a very low P/E Ratio of 15, no debt, and strong growth potential). This is bottom fishing and it will be interesting to see if they continue to grow and go back up to the prices of their hay day.

A good time period to be looking for sale prices is in the middle of a recession. By the time our economy has been in a recession for 6 months, you will KNOW beyond a shadow of a doubt that we are in a recession and that is when the public outcry will cause the slow wheels of government to start turning toward helping the situation (lowering interest rates) and individual businesses will have time to start reducing their inventories, laying off workers (to cut expenses), etc. Therefore, in the next 6 to 12 months after we are officially in a recession, the country should start coming out of the recession. But at that 6 month point the share price of even a very strong "blue chip" company will be at its lowest. This is the time to snatch up some good buys. Essential industries such as food and drink, gasoline, alcoholic beverages, etc. will hardly be effected by a recession, but non-essentials like automobiles, appliances, etc. will have greatly lowered stock prices. You will need excess money not necessary for your immediate living needs and you will need the patience to wait for the recession to end. But this method will create better then average profit for you.

Fifth, you have to put all this information together, look at it logically, and make a decision. Although it may seem difficult to you to make that decision, you really have only two choices: this is a fantastic deal so I will buy some stock _or_ there is a problem with this investment so I think I will pass on it this time. Even if you do decide to pass, you might want to make a mental note and keep checking on this company which attracted you in the first place. See what another three months brings (is it getting better, staying the same, or getting worse). Remember that any investment decision is not cut in granite - - you are allowed to change your mind as circumstances change.

Keep in mind that, at any one time, the vast majority of stocks will not be "good buys". In fact, there might not be any good buys at all during a certain time period. Therefore, have the patience to keep watching and waiting for the right time. Then, when that right time comes, be ready to invest as large an amount as you feel you can comfortably afford.

Do not follow herd psychology and buy what some brokers are suggesting. They, unfortunately, are strongly influenced by what other brokers and analysts are saying rather than what the company is actually doing. Thus, one analyst predicts slightly lower earnings for a particular company over the next quarter and suddenly all the brokers and fund managers are selling that stock. Then, when that company's earnings go up instead of down, they are buying that stock again but at a higher price. Remember that the analyst can benefit financially from that bad prediction.

Your final decision on any investment must be based on _PRICE VS GROWTH AND RISK_. That is, the price you are paying compared with the potential growth of that price and the potential risk of losing it all. Having considered all of the facts, are you willing to pay $500 (or whatever amount) for what you think could be a 250% growth in value over the coming year OR the possible loss of the entire $500? With the facts you have found, do you feel comfortable doing this? If not, do not invest. If you lose the entire amount, is it going to hurt your families day to day living? Do not

feel that you have to invest in something right now. You can wait until the facts do make you feel comfortable. In the meantime, you can be using our previous method and investing a few dollars each month into stock that is very safe and having a high growth rate every year.

Always remember that you have the necessary intelligence to collect and weigh all of the data for yourself. As we mentioned before, some people find it easiest to weigh the information if it is written out in a list form. Some people can actually keep all of these facts in their heads. Some people have found that it helps to keep a folder on any industry or company that they become interested in. They cut out articles or make notes to keep in the files. Whatever method you use for keeping track of all the details, it is important to consider every single detail when making your decision. If one detail does not feel right, then wait.

Suppose you decided to and then actually bought some low priced stock only to see the price drop even more rather than increasing? Look at your research again. If you looked it over carefully before, chances are that you made the right decision and the price will eventually turn around. If it does not start to climb, or something very negative that has long-term effects is recently disclosed, or if the value stays flat (no growth there), you will need to sell (see next chapter). But if you still feel that all of the information is telling you this was a good investment, then buy more! You will be buying at bargain prices for future growth. Particularly where international events are concerned, you might have to wait several months for things to start happening and end up with huge growth in only the last 6 months before a decline sets in. In other words, knowledge, patience and perseverance is still the name of the game.

How about a couple of examples to show you what we have done lately using this method? A recent example is Apple Computer. We all know that Apple was the leader in PC development. However, when the founder, Steve Jobs (management), left the company, things went down hill quickly. The turning point for us personally was when Jobs again took over the management of Apple. At that point, we were looking at strong management (so long as he stayed), poor past financials but with three consecutively profitable quarters after years of losses, these profits coming from the core business rather than from the selling of assets (learned from the financials), three quarters of cutting back on expenses, impressive new products coming out, and a reasonable price of $20 a share. We bought. Each share is now worth $38. However, if Jobs leaves, we probably would sell quickly.

Another example is Chrysler Corporation in the late 1970's to early 1980's. Things had gotten so bad for them that they had to be bailed out by the government or become insolvent. Then they started cutting costs, their earnings grew over a number of quarters, they were introducing new innovative cars and trucks, and the price of a share was low. Yes, they had a good history even with all of this, but the deciding factors were Iacocca, Iacocca, Iacocca. Management can at times make all the difference in a company. Iacocca, just like Eisner at Disney or Jobs at Apple, could and did turn the company around through his strong salesmanship, his charismatic personality, and an autocratic yet healthy sovereignty.

Now is a good time to explain **HOW to jump in**. This is actually the easy part. Once you have decided what stock to buy, you will need to make the purchase through a **broker**. However, not all brokers are created equal! If you have already read "Building Your Financial Portfolio On $25 A Month", you know that we told you to buy just one share through a discount broker that handles one-share purchases and then buy the rest of the shares directly from certain companies that offer direct cash purchase (to avoid broker fees). That is fine for long-term (5 or more years) but not for short-term jumping-in-and-out-of-the-market-at-the-right-time investments.

Instead, you need to make your entire purchase at one time in order to benefit from the low price. Therefore, you will need to find a discount broker who deals in purchases of small amounts (most brokers require a purchase of at least $1,000). At the current time, we know that First Allied Securities (1-800-448-0408) and Quick and Reilly (1-800-221-5220) are doing these smaller transactions. However, keep in mind that, unfortunately, brokerages do have the option of changing their minds at a moments notice so, before signing on the dotted line, make sure they are still doing small transactions. You will be paying a much smaller fee of $25 to $40 for a single transaction (per company) for the first 99 to 1,000 shares because you are making your own decisions. You must pay for your purchase by the 5th business day after the trade and you should receive your security or legal proof by the 5th business day after the transaction.

A quick note about online transactions. For those of you who are computer literate, there are currently about 80 investment companies online with some offering extremely low prices. However, an online company is like a phone marketing company in that it could be a false front. Anyone can set up a web site, rake in a lot of money in 30 days, and then "close their doors". You could be left with nothing. As when dealing with any business, look for familiar names that you know have been in business for years. Do not simply believe them if they tell you they have been in business for 20 years - - check them out first. However, again be aware that most of even the well-known online brokerages will not accept anything under a $1,000 investment. If you have a limited budget, check out their minimum investment first.

Unfortunately, we have found that virtually every broker will try to discourage you from making your own decisions. In our newsletter, "Common Sense Portfolio", we try to keep our readers up to date on what is happening including if certain brokerages have changed their practices and are no longer making small purchases. In order to get up to date information, we phone the different brokerages as just ordinary citizens asking them to do a small transaction for us. Quite often we have found that brokers will give the caller a very difficult time when they realize that you have never done this before. They will try to coerce you into buying more then you can afford or even buying into one of their mutual funds. Remember that brokers are salespeople (that is what they are hired to do) and, therefore, it is in their best interests to have you purchase a mutual fund where they can get steady monthly income from you instead of a one-time transaction fee. Bobbie (being female) has even found it sometimes necessary to firmly state (and pronouncing each word very clearly), "I want to make this purchase, will you do it or not?! This requires a yes or no answer." And, yes, even we have occasionally been mislead by a broker so do not believe everything they tell you unless you can verify it with other sources and get it in writing! Of course, their "writing" is so filled with legalese that you still may not fully understand what they are doing to you.

For instance, it is very important that you tell any broker you deal with that you are to be the "owner of record" meaning that the company you are investing in will list you as the stock holder rather than the brokerage firm. This will guarantee that you receive the quarterly and annual reports and the share holder voting right. This allows you to keep a close eye on the company and get the information you will need to decide when you must sell the stock. You can still have the company (not the broker) hold your shares instead of having to get a safety deposit box for them. It is a common practice for the broker to not offer this "owner of record" form for you to sign and thus keep control of your account. Or you may have blissfully signed all the forms the broker gave you (without having read them carefully) and given him the authority to actively trade your shares, i.e. manage your portfolio for you.

Even though you do not keep the actual shares in your home, you will be receiving quarterly and annual reports directly from the company you invested in (not the broker). For tax purposes as well as your own information, it is important to keep track of this information. Some people, being very well organized, have an office in their house with filing cabinets where everything is in its own folder and in alphabetical order. That's nice. But what is absolutely mandatory is that you have a folder put where you will always know its location and deposit everything you get into that folder. When April 15th approaches, you will have the necessary information to take to your CPA or tax preparer.

Every year you will have to pay taxes on your dividends, even if you have them reinvested into more stock, because this is income for you. You should receive a 1099 from the company for any dividends paid or reinvested. Where it really gets tricky and we suggest that you go to a professional is when you decide to sell any stock. Upon sale of the stock, you will show a taxable gain assuming you made a profit. Financial decisions have to be made as to which shares you sold, the ones you bought two years ago or the ones you bought last month, and the professionals have the computer programs available to decide which will benefit you tax wise.

Speaking of **income taxes**, we are often asked about tax-sheltered investments. First, please be aware that every year the IRS disallows most so-called tax-sheltered investments. Second, the companies that are allowed the status of being tax-shelters are given that status by the government because they are continually losing money anyway (such as dry wells, dead cattle, etc.). Do not try to avoid taxes. Assuming that you are looking to make money, it is better to invest in a company that will give you the highest growth in the value of your stock rather than in a company trying to stay afloat. In fact, the tax write off you would get from the money lost in this type of investment would be very tiny compared with the added money in your pocket (even after taxes) from a huge profit.

For some of you, watching the market every day will be fun. This makes investing more exciting but potentially more dangerous for you then for the person who does not want to bother with all of this. The individual who is bored with all this financial talk will find several good investments that they never have to worry about selling. When making very safe long-term investments, owning stock in no more than 6 different companies is ample **diversification**.

However, if you find the stock market fun and exciting, you run the risk of wanting to be very active, buying into more and more businesses, riskier and riskier companies, and jumping in and out faster and faster. You cannot and will not make money doing this unless you recently found a good buy on a crystal ball. Even using this method of investing in trends for quick results, you should have most of your money in very safe and long-term investments.

Do not try to keep track of more then two or three different companies in your short-term investing or you run the risk of losing track of what is happening and not selling at the appropriate time.

Although it is true that the riskier a company is, the higher your return should be, this only applies if the company succeeds. The fact is that the vast majority of the highly risky companies do not succeed and you could end up losing everything. And if you like the excitement of buying and selling every day, be aware that your broker will be very happy raking in all of those transaction fees. It often takes six months for a company to "spring" ahead. Most brokers feel that the riskier your portfolio is, the more investments you should have, believing that, if half your stock holdings fail, you need the other half to keep you from losing everything. But very few people in this world are excellent jugglers (and you must be excellent, not just good). So keep a small number of investments, both long-term safe ones and short-term riskier ones, that you can comfortably keep track of and only the risky ones you can afford to lose without going bankrupt financially or emotionally.

Contrary to what you might think, a business does not and cannot change overnight. Some may change faster then others, but they all (each and every one) need some time to show results. When you finally make that million, it is only in retrospect that it seems like it was overnight. Again, patience is the word. But how much patience?

The purpose of long-term investing is to find businesses that are so strong and safe that, no matter what happens (almost), you do not have to worry about finding the right time to sell your interest. But we are talking about short-term investing with companies that may not be as strong or as safe making it very necessary to sell your stock before it becomes so devalued that you cannot sell it for what you paid for it.

By now you should have invested either in a particularly good company within a certain growing industry or in an especially good company (separate from its sector) showing great potential growth. Now instead of sitting back and relaxing, it is time to watch the news, the market, the industry, and your company daily for signs of distress. In other words, when do you jump out of your short-term investment.

6. When To "Jump Out"

In order to maximize your profit, you must not only buy when the price is low, you must be able to judge when the price of the stock is near its highest peak. None of us are mind-readers and able to foretell the exact day to sell, but there are things to look for when deciding if this growth is near its high point. It is important to not be greedy about profit. Why waste your time regretting having sold your stock a month too early when you could be using that month to find your next great investment?

The right time to sell stock will vary according to the economic climate, world events, our national events, occurrences within each industry and each company, as well as your own financial status and plans. But the clues you will be looking for in your daily research will be the same for every company you own part of.

Before getting started, consider your own financial status and plans. That is, you should not have invested more money in this plan then you can afford to lose without suffering on the part of you or your family. But you also need to consider what your future plans are. As we have defined short-term investing as being for 18 months or longer, you need to know what you will be doing at least 18 months from now (as much as is humanly possible anyway).

Are you going to have certain commitments that you must meet such as a child starting college or will you need several thousand dollars to buy a new car? Obviously, you must plan these things *before* doing any short-term purchases. But what many people forget is to continue this planning while holding these investments. That is, think ahead and mark your calendar if necessary so that you will have at least 18 months notice of when you are going to need a large sum of money. Thus, if you know that in that amount of time you are going to need $15,000 for a child's college expenses, you can watch for spikes in the value of your stock. For example, let's say that it is summertime and you know that the next Fall you will need this money. During the coming months the price of any particular stock will have slight variations; it will continue upward for a time, drop down a bit, and then continue upward. Knowing that these are normal fluctuations, you would want to make the necessary sale during an upturn rather than during one of those downward spikes. As a rule, these would not be large price changes but could mean that you would make $2 or $3 more on each share that you hold. However, if you have become involved in high-tech stocks with their extreme volatility or price fluctuations, be aware that their share price can change by as much as $10 or even more in one day.

However, when it comes to selling an investment, what we are most concerned about is a major change that means the value of your stock is going to start declining for, quite possibly, a very long time. What signs and events must you watch for?

A. The most important thing to watch for is a destructive **recession**. In this case, you will be looking for a minimum of 3 economic indicators. A short-term cycle such as holiday shopping or presidential elections should have only a temporary effect on the market. But what are these 3 major indicators?

1. Rise in Interest Rates: If you hear in the news that inflation is on the rise, you can expect an increase in interest rates to follow rather quickly. Besides the increase you would see in your own monthly budget for groceries, gas, etc., you would also hear about a continuing rise (over two to three months time) in the Consumer Price Index. At this point, as you know, the Federal Reserve would start increasing interest rates making the borrowing of money too expensive for companies that wanted to expand. If you see interest rates rise 2 or 3 times, it may be time to get out of that company that had great plans to build new plants and hire more workers and go back into safe long-term investing.

2. Rise in Unemployment: A rise in the unemployment rate means companies are having to cut back due to people buying fewer of their products and means we may be headed into a recession. This factor will particularly effect non-essential industries such as automobile, building, appliance, computer, and other durable goods that last for many years before needing to be replaced by the consumer. This will also effect so-called discretionary (not necessary but fun or convenient) spending in such areas as recreation and restaurant businesses.

Either a rise in interest rates or a rise in the unemployment rate or both at the same time would have an immediate effect on the stock market. However, you do not want to jump to quickly only to find out it was just a correction rather than a slump into recession. But if you see the next item occurring at the same time, then jump quickly.

3. Drop in Earnings: If you see earnings for most companies in the stock market dropping, even slowly, at the same time that you see a rise in the interest rate and a rise in the unemployment rate, it is time to sell your short-term holding immediately. Do not wait a couple of months to see what happens because our economy cannot handle all three of these things at one time and a recession will quickly follow. Of course, we do not know just how long that recession will last, but that does not matter to us when deciding whether to sell our short-term investments. Yes, when we are at the depth of the recession, you will want to be looking for good buys knowing that business will soon start improving. But for now, just sell and reap your rewards!

B. However, there are other events to watch for that may effect only your particular investment rather than our whole economy. These episodes could mean that you should sell any short-term holdings you have in that individual company.

1. Is an international event going to have an adverse effect on your company? Is your stock heavily owned by foreign interests that could decide to sell off their shares causing the price of your shares to collapse? Is another country with a much lower wage scale building up competition for your company? Although these kinds of things would happen over a longer period of time (perhaps several months), you need to spot these as quickly as possible in order to sell your holdings before the value is severely effected.

2. Has congress passed new legislation creating higher taxes for the industry group you have invested in? Or have they passed new laws effecting your industry? The advent of pollution control laws had a devastating effect on many chemical, lumber, etc. companies. These actions may be more difficult to base a sell decision on because the taxes may not be large enough to have a big effect. A new law controlling certain manufacturing methods may be played up in the media as being devastating and end up causing only slight inconvenience for the involved companies while they adjust their mode of operation.

IMPORTANT: Do not stop reading the companies financial reports and annual reports just because you now own part of it. It is more important then ever to be on the lookout for problems that would be visible in their quarterly and annual reports.

3. Is the company you are invested in showing signs of distress? That is, has the company recently discontinued dividends? Are their earnings dropping? High or continually growing earnings for the stock market as a whole do not necessarily mean that your company is still growing. A drop in just one quarter could be a holiday cycle, a bookkeeping adjustment such as a merger, or other normal event. However, if their earnings continue to drop, they are having a severe problem.

4. Has their debt risen too high? High debt will cut into their earnings as they make ever increasing payments on that debt.

5. Has the company stopped putting more money into research and development? If the budget for this area is staying flat or, even worse, decreasing, then this company is having a serious financial or management problem. That is, you know that without R & D there is no growth. If this cut back is a financial decision, are there other signs that they are attempting to correct these problems? If this cut back is a management problem, is it a new CEO that is making bad business decisions?

6. Is the management about to change? If the president of a company leaves or even dies, has he already chosen and trained a replacement or will the Board of Directors need to search for someone else? Will this change be good or bad for the company? Are other key management people suddenly leaving for other companies? Are management people selling off large portions of their holdings in the company? Is the business being bought out by another and, if so, is the new parent company knowledgeable in this industry or are they buying the competition just to get rid of it?

7. Is the price of the stock in this particular company continuously dropping. Hopefully, you will have spotted the above signs before the value of the stock has been effected very much. But do not be fooled by a price correction in this particular company. All stock values will fluctuate. On the Value Line graph you will not see a perfectly straight line headed up. The line will show jags in it. However, make sure that the low point of each correction ends higher then the low point of the last correction (a jagged line but continually going upward). If the price drops $2, then goes up $1, then drops $2, then goes up $1 (showing a jagged but dropping price) it could

be time to sell unless there are other very strong reasons that make you believe this is a temporary correction in the stock price. Again, do not follow herd psychology. As we have already said, brokers and analysts can have their own reasons for causing prices to fall that have nothing to do with the actual company involved.

C. Finally, if certain conditions make it necessary to sell your short-term investment, commonly referred to as "take the money and run", put your profit into safer, long-term, high yield investments such as we discuss in *Building Your Financial Portfolio On $25 A Month (Or Less)*. Keep in mind that the "blue chip" stocks we would normally use for safe long-term investing can also be used for short-term investing. For example, if you invested in something like Coca-Cola that may have short down turns but, overall, will continue to increase in value, you can sell that at any point you wish. If the price goes up $20 in 6 months, you can sell it. If the price goes down $20 in 6 months, you can hold onto it knowing that it will gain that $20 back fairly quickly.

Another example is the one we used on page 6 about Exxon. Suppose that something had happened to take Eric's mind off of his investing for awhile and, therefore, he did not sell it 18 months later when it was at a high price. Shortly after that, the Exxon Valdez incident occurred and the stock price drop drastically. Would we have lost everything because he waited too long? Well, as the saying goes, you haven't lost anything if you haven't sold it. But more importantly, we would not have lost anything because this was a strong company and had gained back all it had lost in value in the next 18 months and continued to go up from there.

In other words, there are different levels of risk that you can take in short-term investing. You can invest in a risky company that you will have to get out of at the right time in order to protect your profits, or you can invest in a relatively safe stock that you might make a smaller profit in by waiting too long to sell but in which you would not actually lose anything. And then there are many different amounts of risk in between these two. Risk only what you are comfortable with.

As with a buying decision, your final selling decision must be based on PRICE VS GROWTH AND RISK. That is, has the priced dropped to a point and the growth potential come to a stop whereby you must sell in order to not risk the profit you have already made? Also, do you still feel comfortable with your investment? Other then the 3 steps in A above, the clues may not be very obvious to you. But if you are feeling very nervous about the situation, then sell your holdings and go back into the safe investments.

Everything in your life is just part of a particular cycle that has a beginning, a middle, and an end. The stock market and even individual companies live the same way. Something will start to happen, continue to have an effect, and then end. And then it starts over again. Good times do not last forever, but neither do the bad times.

Do not waste your time on hindsight and fret "If only I had bought it one week earlier" or "If only I had waited and sold one month later". This does no one any good. Instead, focus on the profit you did make. This is the time to get ready for your next foray into short-term, high yield investing. After all, this is money that you did not even have to work for. At least, we hope you didn't consider this hard work. We hope you can relax and enjoy this new venture and truly appreciate the large increase in your money that our system of government and free market has allowed you to partake of.

The **HOW** part of jumping out of your investment is also easy. If you have decided to sell your stock, the first thing you must do is call the company directly and ask if they are doing a "buy back". Depending on the economic situation, quite a few companies will be doing this at any one time. With a buy back, the company will buy your stock directly from you, usually at a premium price (slightly more then the open market price) and will quite often pay the broker fees.

However, if there is no buy back going on, the next important thing to remember is to use a discount broker and shop for prices. The discount broker you used for the purchase may have raised his prices since then or other brokers have drastically dropped their prices so check out their fees again before selling. Also, be aware that once you have done a transaction with a broker, you may be eligible to use their online services which can have even cheaper rates. But do shop around for prices.

7. In Conclusion

We have tried to keep all of this information brief and to the point. As you have seen, we believe in spelling steps out very carefully so as not to confuse anyone. Although we cannot reiterate all of this information, there are certain points that it is important for you to keep in mind.

Keep most of your money in safe long-term investments that will have continued good growth. If you are willing to take the time to become a specialist in certain industries and to do the required research, put some of your money into short-term investments that have the potential of huge growth. Never invest more money then you can afford to lose without regret and remorse. And share this information with your family, friends, and co-workers so that everyone will have the knowledge necessary to participate in your stock market for the sake of your country's future as well as your own financial future.

May you live long and prosper!

GLOSSARY

Assets - Things that a company can convert to cash including cash, accounts receivable, and inventory.

Beta - A number system used to describe how much a stock or stocks fluctuate from the overall market.

Bond - Issued by a government to cover their debt and has a fixed interest rate and fixed maturity date.

Buy-Back - A company decides to buy back outstanding shares that they can then sell again at a future date.

Closed-End Fund - A fund with a fixed number of shares as opposed to an open-end mutual fund.

Consumer Price Index - Issued by the Labor Department monthly to show changes in the cost of living.

Dividend - An amount determined by the Board of Directors of a company to be paid to each share holder per each share held.

Dow Jones Industrial Average - An average of the 30 largest U.S. industrial companies. The Transportation Average includes 20 companies and the Utility Average includes 15 companies.

Federal Reserve Board - Regulates certain banks and sets national monetary policy, makes loans from one bank to another and sets the interest rate charged for these loans.

Gross National Product (GNP) - An estimate of the total goods and services created by U.S. companies which is an indicator of the economic strength or weakness.

Interest Rate - Additional amount to be paid back above the actual loan amount.

Liabilities - Things owed by a company including accounts payable, taxes, wages, and debt.

Money Supply - Calculations of the Federal Reserve used to indicate the money supply, i.e. if it grows faster than overall economic growth, inflation can follow.

New York Stock Exchange Composite - Average of all the common stocks on the NYSE.

Options - A stock holder can put in an option order with a broker to buy or sell 100 shares of stock when it reaches a certain price.

Owner of Record - Who, broker or individual, has control of shares of stock.

Price/Earnings (P/E) Ratio - The price per share of stock divided by the earnings per year. Indicates if the price is too high for what the earnings are (or too low or in line) and varies from one industry to anther.

Recession - The GNP, adjusted for the rate of inflation, declines for two quarters in a row.

Short-Term Investing - Investing money for up to four years though usually for about 18 months. As opposed to long-term investing of at least 5 years but preferably 10 years or more.

Split - The Board of Directors of a company increases the number of shares outstanding. 2-for-1 split, your 1 share is now 2 shares, 3-for-1 split, your 1 share is now 3 shares, etc.

SPECIAL OFFER

Common Sense Portfolio Newsletter

a newsletter by the authors of
***Building Your Financial Portfolio On $25 A Month
(Or Less)***

and

Adding To Your Financial Portfolio

By popular request, Eric and Bobbie Christensen are now providing you monthly information on the safest stock investments with the best growth potential. Each issue contains information on specific companies that has been specially picked to meet all of the investing criteria set forth in their books.

To accompany ***Building Your Financial Portfolio On $25 A Month (Or Less)***, the company chosen will have a long-term history of excellent growth and safety along with automatic reinvestment of dividends and a cash purchase plan to avoid future stock broker fees. To accompany ***Adding To Your Financial Portfolio***, a company will be chosen that has been analyzed for risk, growth potential, and timeliness for your short-term investing. You will get the specific information you need to decide for yourself.

Every monthly issue will include up-to-date information on discount brokers, current events impacting your financial decisions and other aspects of stock market investing that you need to know.

BIBLIOGRAPHY

Brutus. Confessions Of A Stockbroker - A Wall Street Diary. Little, Brown & Co., Boston, 1971

Carlson, Charles B. Buying Stocks Without A Broker. McGraw-Hill, Inc., NY, 1992.

Investor's Business Daily. Guide To The Markets. John Wiley & Sons, Inc., NY, 1996.

Lehmann, Michael B. Using The Wall Street Journal. Business One Irwin, IL, 1993.

Lowenstein, Roger. Buffett, The Making Of An American Capitalist. Random House, NY, 1995.

O'Neil, William J. How To Make Money In Stocks. McGrraw-Hill, Inc., NY, 1995.

Rosenberg, Jerry M. Inside The Wall Street Journal. Macmillan Publishing Co., NY, 1982.

Sease, Douglas & Prestbo, John. Barron's Guide To Making Investment Decisions. Prentice Hall, NJ, 1994.

Sivy, Michael. Rules of Investing - How To Pick Stocks Like A Pro. Warner Books, Inc., NY, 1996.

Spitz, William T. Get Rich Slowly. MacMillan, NY, 1992.

Walden, Gene. <u>The 100 Best Stocks To Own In America</u>. Longman Financial Services Publishing, 1997.

Whitney, Russ. <u>Building Wealth</u>. Simon & Schuster, NY, 1994.

Also by Bobbie and Eric Christensen

Building Your Financial Portfolio
On $25 A Month (Or Less) $12.95

Adding To Your Financial Portfolio $12.95

Common Sense Portfolio Newsletter
(12 monthly issues) $21.00

Also by Bobbie Christensen

Getting A Free Education: The Key To Your
Dream Job $11.95

Getting Your Dream Life: Career, Sex & Leisure $11.95

Add $1.50 per order for shipping and handling

To order, call 1-800-929-7889 (Mastercard & Visa accepted)

or mail check or money order to:
Effective Living Publishing, P.O.Box 232233,
Sacramento, CA 95823

Prices guaranteed through 12/99